TO:

FROM:

DATE:

from where I stand

A 30-DAY JOURNEY WITH WOMEN OF THE BIBLE

Shanna Noel
& Sherri Gragg

INTRODUCTION

The creation account in Genesis is so beautifully written that it almost feels like poetry.

In the beginning God created the heavens and the earth.
Now the earth was formless and empty, darkness was over the surface
of the deep, and the Spirit of God was hovering over the waters."

GENESIS 1:1–2 NIV

From there, the writer of Genesis gives us a step-by-step account of the Creator's work, each development more complex, more magnificent, than the last.

Light is created and then separated from the darkness. Next, the divine hand gathers the waters into one place, making room for His subsequent creation—the sky.

He corrals the waters again, making room for the land. Then, He brings forth vegetation on the land before setting the sun, moon, and stars in the sky.

He fills the sea with aquatic creatures and the sky with birds before moving on to fill the land with countless varieties of animals.

He gathers a bit of dust together, breathes into it, and makes man to serve as a caretaker for all He has created.

Then, finally, the Creator has one last act to complete, His grand finale—woman.

Most translations tell us that God made woman to be a "helper" for Adam, but this word falls a bit short. The Hebrew word here is, *ēzer*, and yes, it does mean "aid," but when we look for where this word appears elsewhere in Scripture, we find, to our surprise, that it often refers to the Creator Himself, the One who comes to our aid in moments of great need and saves us. (See Psalms 30:10 & 54:4.)

It is a powerful word, less akin to a servant than a superhero—one who rides in to save the day.

Does this shock you? If so, you have come to the right place. In this study, we will ponder the women's stories God chose to include in Scripture. Together we will ask: Why this woman? Why this story? What is God trying to tell us about His heart for women?

It is our prayer that through this study you might more clearly see yourself as He sees you ...

Crowned with dignity and honor. A beautiful creation, formed by His hands with a purpose.

Loved ... endlessly, extravagantly, loved by God.

CONTENTS

DAY 1

Eve

Eve's life had been quiet for so long.

Once, a lifetime ago, it had not been so. When her boys, Cain and Abel, were small, her days were filled with the sounds of childhood.

Shouts of laughter. The stampede of bare feet as they chased each other in their play. The low whispers that drifted to her through the darkness as the brothers planned the next day's adventures from their sleeping mats.

But as they grew into young men, their relationship began to change.

Laughter gave way to harsh words and tears. Instead of moving toward each other in friendship, her sons pulled away from each other, each wary of bridging the distance between them. At night, an angry silence fell over the tent as they turned their backs to each other from their sleeping mats.

Eve knew things were bad between her sons, but how could she have ever imagined the horror that was to come?

Abel's blood soaking into the cursed earth, his young life cut short by his own brother's hand.

Cain lost, too, driven away from home and family by his crime.

In one breathtaking stroke, Eve was forced to bury one son and watch the other walk out of her life forever.

Somehow, she opened her eyes that next morning. Somehow, she took her next breath. Somehow, she kept putting one foot in front of the other.

And the quiet descended, carried on the back of grief. In the silence of loss, life slipped by, day by day, month by month, year after year.

The loss of Cain and Abel was an ocean of pain that seemed to stretch endlessly between Eve and her husband Adam—too vast to chart, too precarious to cross. Until, somehow, a lifetime later, Adam and Eve drifted nearer each other, close enough to reach for the comfort of each other's arms across the years of loss. It was the beginning of healing, the first stirring of resurrection. The advent of new life.

Now, the silent years of mourning have drawn to an end.

Eve groans in agony as a contraction washes over her. With the next wave of pain, she cries out, and a moment later another, fainter cry, takes the place of her own.

Through laughter and joyful tears, Eve reaches down to lift her newborn son to her chest with trembling hands. She holds him near, and whispers his name for the first time

"Seth."

The weary mother laughs in wonder as the baby boy's face wrinkles in fury and his cry grows louder. Once again, the sounds of life have come to her tent, filling the emptiness.

Banishing the quiet of grief and loss.

Tears have given way to laughter, and the sound of bare feet running in play won't be far behind. At night, a baby's cry will once again pierce the stillness of her tent, accompanied by whispered prayers of gratitude.

For at last, new life has come.

Scripture Reading

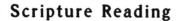

Read the Scripture below of the account describing Eve's loss of her first two sons, and the miracle of the moment when, after so many years of grief, God filled her arms with her third son, Seth.

Genesis 4:8–16, 25–26 NRSVA

Cain said to his brother Abel, "Let us go out to the field." And when they were in the field, Cain rose up against his brother Abel and killed him. Then the Lord said to Cain, "Where is your brother Abel?" He said, "I do not know; am I my brother's keeper?" And the Lord said, "What have you done? Listen, your brother's blood is crying out to me from the ground! And now you are cursed from the ground, which has opened its mouth to receive your brother's blood from your hand. When you till the ground, it will no longer yield to you its strength; you will be a fugitive and a wanderer on the earth." Cain said to the Lord, "My punishment is greater than I can bear! Today You have driven me away from the soil, and I shall be hidden from Your face; I shall be a fugitive and a wanderer on the earth, and anyone who meets me may kill me." Then the Lord said to him, "Not so! Whoever kills Cain will suffer a sevenfold vengeance." And the Lord put a mark on Cain, so that no one who came upon him would kill him. Then Cain went away from the presence of the Lord and settled in the land of Nod, east of Eden ...

Adam knew his wife again, and she bore a son and named him Seth, for she said, "God has appointed for me another child instead of Abel, because Cain killed him." To Seth also a son was born, and he named him Enosh. At that time people began to invoke the name of the Lord.

Let's Review

All humans make mistakes. Most of us fall for the accuser's lies at one point or another. Sometimes, it seems Eve has been judged ruthlessly for her own moment of weakness in the garden. Have you ever taken a moment to ask yourself why that is? What are your thoughts about this?

Eve lost both of her sons in one horrifying, heartbreaking moment. One son was lost to death, the other to exile for his crime. How has this contemplation of her loss given you more compassion for her? Conversely, how does having compassion for Eve allow you to possibly offer more compassion to yourself when you fall into temptation?

Ultimately, today's reading is a story about the struggle between life and death—a theme we see woven throughout the whole of Scripture. Where have you felt this struggle in your own life?

Application

If we approach the creation narrative as a story about Adam and Eve, we not only set Eve up for an unfair share of blame, but we also miss the bigger, more important struggle at place.

Genesis 2 is about more than a love story gone wrong; it is about the larger conflict woven throughout the entire Bible—the conflict between life and death.

From the moment the serpent slithered into the garden, the battle lines were drawn. On one side was a loving Creator who fashioned creation with such abundance and magnificence that our finite human understanding is left staggering beneath the weight of its glory.

On the other side is Satan, "the adversary," who is driven endlessly to destroy all that has been fashioned by the Creator's hand. His approach of Eve in the garden is strategic. She is the crescendo of creation, God's joyous crowning glory on all He has made. She is also "the life-giver," which is the Hebrew translation of her name.

Ever the cruel terrorist, Satan strikes—infecting God's precious creation with death through his deception of the one who was meant to bring forth new life into it.

Eve's conversation with Satan is the first time we hear her speak in Scripture. Her words are recorded only three other times. The next occasion is found in Genesis 3:13, when God confronts her about her disobedience. Here, her words capture her efforts to rid herself of her unbearable shame by casting blame upon the serpent, Satan, who had deceived her.

When Eve speaks again, in Genesis 4:1, it is in the weary aftermath of childbirth as the sweat still clings to her brow and tears fill her eyes. Life has been hard for Eve. The bliss of Eden is far behind. Each day has been filled with the grueling work of survival, carried on beneath the burden of guilt and shame.

Every birth is a miracle, but this birth, the first one, is even more so because it is a moment of profound redemption. That day in the garden when Eve fell, death had come. Now, through her, so had life. She pulls her newborn son, Cain, to her breast and says of him, "I have gotten a man with the help of the Lord" (Genesis 4:1 ESV).

Eve's final words to us are spoken years later, long after she has buried her second son, Abel, murdered by his own brother, Cain. Eve, the "Life Giver," has one last declaration to make as she brings her third son, Seth, into the world. "God has granted me another child in place of Abel" (Genesis 4:25 NIV).

Against all odds. Despite every mistake and in defiance of each regret . . .

Life wins.

And this is the love story of Scripture from beginning to end: a loving God gives life. The accuser attacks, bringing death. For a time, it seems all hope is gone.

But God always has the last word.

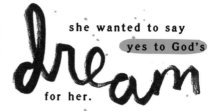

she wanted to say yes to God's dream for her.

Prompt

Have you ever experienced a season in which it seems "death" has won? This may not necessarily refer to a physical death, but to any loss that seemed to have had the final say-so in your life. If so, write about what you learned during that season. If you are in the middle of this dark struggle now, write a prayer, pouring out your sorrow and hurt to God.

Dig Deeper

Romans 8:18–21
Romans 8:22–25
Romans 8:26–30

DAY 2

Sarai

Wife. Mother.

These were the identities Sarai's culture offered her. As a young teenager, she had dutifully fulfilled the role of wife, but the role of mother eluded her.

Each month, she waited in expectation for the telltale signs that a baby was on the way, only to find her hope pushed to the next month. And the next. At first, she was disappointed, but as the months and years stretched by with no child, disappointment surely gave way to despair.

For decades, Sarai sat on the sidelines of motherhood as her neighbors' bellies swelled with new life. Wistfully, she watched as their arms filled with babies, and then, as those babies grew faster than the reeds along the banks of the nearby Balīkh River in her hometown of Harran.

From the quiet, tidy stillness of her home, she listened as boys and girls ran past outside, their voices calling out to each other in play.

How many nights did Sarai cry herself to sleep, begging God for a child before years of emptiness robbed her supplications of their fervor, and hope died completely?

Then, when her neighbors' children had grown old enough to have children, even grandchildren, of their own, Sarai's tidy, quiet, *empty* life was interrupted—*upended* even—by God's call and promise.

"Go," the command came, "from your country, your people, and your father's household ... ."

Words that cut like a knife, severing Sarai from all she knew, and more importantly, from the safety and provision that life afforded her. God didn't even bother to get specific about where to go, simply saying that He would show them on the way.

But His command came with something better than a relocation plan; it came with a promise.

"I will make you into a great nation, and I will bless you. . . ."

A great nation?

But Sarai was old now, far past the years of childbearing. How could God bring a great nation from her husband when her womb had yet to produce one small child?

A flicker of hope. One wrinkled hand instinctively falling to rest on her lower abdomen. *Could it be?*

Wife. Mother. These were the only identities afforded her by her culture, and although God would grant Sarai's desire to be a mother, He deemed her *more*.

*Sarai, the strong . . .

Sarai, the blessed . . .

Sarai, the beloved, crowned with dignity . . .

Made in the image of God.

*In Genesis 17:15, God changes Sarai's name to "Sarah," which means, "a fortification."

Scripture Reading

Read the Scripture below for the Bible's introduction of Sarai and to learn more about God's promise to Sarai.

Genesis 11:29–12:5 NIV

Abram and Nahor both married. The name of Abram's wife was Sarai, and the name of Nahor's wife was Milkah; she was the daughter of Haran, the father of both Milkah and Iskah. Now Sarai was childless because she was not able to conceive.

Terah took his son Abram, his grandson Lot son of Haran, and his daughter-in-law Sarai, the wife of his son Abram, and together they set out from Ur of the Chaldeans to go to Canaan. But when they came to Harran, they settled there.

Terah lived 205 years, and he died in Harran.

The LORD had said to Abram, "Go from your country, your people and your father's household to the land I will show you.

I will make you into a great nation,
   and I will bless you;
I will make your name great,
   and you will be a blessing.
I will bless those who bless you,
   and whoever curses you I will curse;
and all peoples on earth
   will be blessed through you."

So Abram went, as the LORD had told him; and Lot went with him. Abram was seventy-five years old when he set out from Harran. He took his wife Sarai, his nephew Lot, all the possessions they had accumulated and the people they had acquired in Harran, and they set out for the land of Canaan, and they arrived there.

Let's Review

Sarai's culture defined her worth by her status as wife and mother. What are some ways our culture seems to define women?

In today's story, we imagine what it must have been like for Sarai to watch her neighbors grow their families when she couldn't. Most of us struggle with feelings of self-doubt as we compare ourselves to others. How have you experienced this?

At the end of our story, Sarai is severed from all she knows in Harran and the provision and protection her home and her husband's family afforded her. Imagine you were in Sarai's place. What emotions might you have experienced? How do you think the situation would have impacted your relationship with God?

Application

Sarai was made in the image of God, and therefore, possessed her own unique identity independent of any other defining characteristics or roles. Her culture, however, offered her no individual identity other than wife and mother.

Sarai dutifully became a bride at a young age, but her secondary cultural identity, that of mother, eluded her.

Of course, Sarai had no power over whether she conceived. Her inability to do so was not a character flaw nor did it diminish her worth as a child of God in any way.

Even so, the cacophony of lesser voices attacking her self-worth as a "barren" woman would have surely been difficult to ignore.

There are countless voices in our lives that seek to tell us who we are, or more often, who we are not. These false standards of "worthiness" inevitably lead to harm. At the very least, we become harried and exhausted as we try to keep up with the images we see on social media—images that are filtered and lives that have been edited to show us a falsified reality with which we will never be able to compete.

So what is the answer?

We need the same thing Sarai needed: we need to know what *God* thinks of us. Listening to what He has to say about our identity in a world that relentlessly tries to define us is a breath of fresh air that leads to joy and freedom!

God's view of us is always gentle and loving, always graced with dignity. We are image bearers of God, loved beyond all measure, precious in His sight.

a flicker of hope

Prompt

Which voices in your world threaten to define your identity? Not sure? Here's a hint: they are the voices that likely leave you feeling "less than." Write a prayer below asking God to heal you from the scars those voices have left behind, then ask Him for ears to hear what He alone has to say about who you are in Him.

Dig Deeper

Psalm 139:13–14
Song of Songs 6:9
Psalm 17:7–9

DAY 3

Hagar, Seen by God

The sun was just breaking over the horizon when Hagar stepped from the tent and into Abraham's camp for the last time. So many years had passed since she was taken from her home in Egypt, sold as a slave to Abraham and his wife, Sarah. She was just a girl then. Now, worn by years of service, she was a woman.

And a mother.

Hagar scanned the yard for Ishmael and spotted him standing next to one of the donkeys, running his long fingers through its mane.

Saying goodbye . . .

Her heart ached for her boy. If only she could change his fate, make him the legitimate son of a first wife and not that of a slave who was made a bride (Genesis 16:1-3) only when her mistress failed to conceive.

For thirteen years, his entire childhood, Ishmael was the treasured firstborn son. Even Sarah doted on him as her own. Then, at the age of ninety, Sarah conceived. She bore a son, Isaac, and for Ishmael, everything changed.

Sarah's heart had grown cold toward Ishmael under the weight of her fierce protection of Isaac's position and inheritance. Eventually, she went to Abraham and demanded he send Hagar and Ishmael away.

The sun rose a bit higher in the sky, warming the cool morning air. Soon, it would beat down on the desert surrounding Beersheba with a savage and relentless heat. Hagar watched as Ishmael shyly moved to his father's side. The hurt on the boy's face was undeniable. Abraham glanced down at him, his own face lined with sorrow, then looked away.

Hagar took a deep breath and then moved toward her husband and son. It was best to begin her travels home toward Egypt before the sun climbed any higher. She wasn't sure which way to go. It had been so long since she had traveled that way.

Abraham placed a satchel of food and a skin of water on her back. She took Ishmael by the hand and began to walk away from the abundance of Abraham's tents and into the barren desert of Beersheba holding tight to her only hope.

God had met her in the wilderness once before.

Many years before when she was young, pregnant with Abraham's baby and running from Sarah's abuse, Hagar had fled into the desert. God found her there, and she named Him, *El Roi*, "the God who sees." (Genesis 16:13 NIV)

He told her to return to Sarah, but He sent her back into bondage with a promise: the child she was carrying would grow into a great nation. God said she was to name him, Ishmael, "God hears."

God sees . . .

God hears . . .

And once again, Hagar held on to hope that He was also a God who saves.

Scripture Reading

Read the passage below for the scriptural account of Hagar and Ishmael wandering in the desert.

Genesis 21:14–21 NIV

Early the next morning Abraham took some food and a skin of water and gave them to Hagar. He set them on her shoulders and then sent her off with the boy. She went on her way and wandered in the Desert of Beersheba.

When the water in the skin was gone, she put the boy under one of the bushes. Then she went off and sat down about a bowshot away, for she thought, "I cannot watch the boy die." And as she sat there, she began to sob.

God heard the boy crying, and the angel of God called to Hagar from heaven and said to her, "What is the matter, Hagar? Do not be afraid; God has heard the boy crying as he lies there. Lift the boy up and take him by the hand, for I will make him into a great nation."

Then God opened her eyes and she saw a well of water. So she went and filled the skin with water and gave the boy a drink.

God was with the boy as he grew up. He lived in the desert and became an archer. While he was living in the Desert of Paran, his mother got a wife for him from Egypt.

Let's Review

Hagar was a slave girl when Sarah gave her to Abraham as a wife so that Sarah might have a son through her. Years later, when Sarah conceived a child of her own, Sarah demanded Abraham send Hagar and Ishmael away. Imagine you are Hagar. What emotions would you experience as you took your only son by the hand and left his home and inheritance for the dangers of the desert and an uncertain future?

When Hagar was young and pregnant with Ishmael and fleeing Sarah's abuse, she had a personal encounter with God after which she named Him, "El-Roi," the God who sees her. In today's Scripture reading, when she and Ishmael are near death in the desert, Scripture tells us God hears Ishmael's cries. How does it make you feel to know that God sees and hears the vulnerable when they have been mistreated by those in power?

Re-read the last paragraph of today's Scripture. What hints do you see there that God kept His promise to Hagar that He would make Ishmael into a "great nation"?

Application

Wouldn't it be much more comfortable if God omitted the less flattering stories about the heroes of faith, like Abraham and Sarah, from Scripture?

Stories like Hagar's challenge us to face dark truths about the men and women we sang songs about as children in Sunday school and whose images we filled in with happy colors after Bible story time.

Hagar was taken into slavery as a child, then forced to marry a man several times her age so that she might conceive a son for her mistress to call her own. While pregnant, she suffered abuse at Sarah's hand (Genesis 16:6). Then, years later, when Sarah miraculously conceived a son of her own, Hagar and her son, Ishmael, were sent into the desert with meager provisions for the journey and an even thinner hope for their future.

These are disheartening truths.

Why did God include Hagar's story? Why not just leave us blissfully ignorant?

Perhaps God preserved her life in Scripture so that we might know that people like Hagar matter to Him so much that He not only bears witness to their suffering, but He also asks us to do the same. God challenges us to not look away from those who suffer injustice and oppression. He asks us to hear their cry when they call.

Living with this kind of godlike awareness isn't easy, but it is an important part of what it means to work to bring His good and just kingdom down to earth (Matthew 6:10).

God met her in the wilderness

Prompt

Write a prayer asking God to give you a heart like His for the vulnerable and oppressed.

Dig Deeper

Proverbs 15:3
Psalm 10:17
Psalm 102:17

DAY 4

Sarah, the Fearful

From the door of her tent, Sarah watched as Hagar and Ishmael prepared to leave. Awkwardly, hesitantly, Ishmael walked to where his father, Abraham, knelt on the ground placing a loaf of bread and a few other provisions for their journey into a sack. Hagar hung back a bit, giving father and son a few final moments alone.

Isaac wrapped chubby toddler fingers into Sarah's robe and tugged before lifting his arms, signaling that he wanted her to pick him up. Sarah bent over slowly, her aged back aching, and lifted the boy to her hip.

Briefly, she nuzzled his cheek and planted soft kisses there before turning her eyes back to the scene before her. The camp was just coming to life in the cool morning air. A few of Abraham's servants herded a large flock of bleating sheep together, preparing to lead them out in search of pasture. Some of her own servants gathered sticks together to start a fire while others grabbed large water jugs before slowly making their way to fetch water for the day.

All around her was abundance, but none more miraculous than the little boy on her hip, the baby of promise born to her in her old age. God had prospered Abraham and Sarah in the years since He commanded them to leave Harran and follow Him into the unknown.

Sarah watched as Hagar lifted her eyes from the dust at her feet and walked to where Abraham and Ishmael were standing. It was time for them to get going before the deadly sun rose any higher in the desert sky. Abraham lifted the bag of provisions and a skin of water to Hagar's back. Ishmael, his face stricken, blinked back tears.

Who is laughing now?

Only a few days before, at the feast celebrating Isaac's weaning, Ishmael had laughed at his little brother in mockery. It was then that Sarah decided he and his mother would have to go. For thirteen years, Ishmael had played the part of favored first son, but now that God had given Isaac to Abraham and Sarah, that role belonged to him.

Sarah was determined to eliminate any threat to Isaac's position and inheritance. *That slave girl's boy would have no part of it.*

Hagar and Ishmael looked at Abraham one last time before making their way to the edge of camp. Beyond that safe space of abundance, spread the endless desert, barren and brutal.

Sarah turned back into the comfort of her tent. They were leaving. She could breathe easily at last.

Scripture Reading

Read the scriptural account below of God's fulfilled promise to Sarah and her treatment of Hagar and Ishmael.

Genesis 21:1–10 NIV

Now the LORD was gracious to Sarah as He had said, and the LORD did for Sarah what He had promised. Sarah became pregnant and bore a son to Abraham in his old age, at the very time God had promised him. Abraham gave the name Isaac to the son Sarah bore him. When his son Isaac was eight days old, Abraham circumcised him, as God commanded him. Abraham was a hundred years old when his son Isaac was born to him.

Sarah said, "God has brought me laughter, and everyone who hears about this will laugh with me." And she added, "Who would have said to Abraham that Sarah would nurse children? Yet I have borne him a son in his old age."

The child grew and was weaned, and on the day Isaac was weaned Abraham held a great feast. But Sarah saw that the son whom Hagar the Egyptian had borne to Abraham was mocking, and she said to Abraham, "Get rid of that slave woman and her son, for that woman's son will never share in the inheritance with my son Isaac."

Let's Review

Re-read the first paragraph of today's Scripture reading. List all the ways you see God's abundance and faithfulness to Sarah in this section.

Look at the second paragraph of the Scripture reading. What task specific to motherhood does Sarah mention that she is granted in her old age? How would you describe her emotions in this portion of our reading?

Read the last sentence of today's Scripture reading. Do you think God's miraculous provision for Sarah made her more generous or less so?

Application

Sarah's joy is almost tangible in the first verses of today's Scripture reading. Sarah will give birth to, and nurse, a son in her old age. She is so awestruck by God's extravagance that she proclaims:

"God has brought me laughter, and everyone who hears about this will laugh with me." And she added, "Who would have said to Abraham that Sarah would nurse children? Yet I have borne him a son in his old age." (Genesis 21:6-7 NIV)

Approximately three years pass between these verses and the ones that conclude our reading, but Sarah's heart is changed so dramatically that it is unrecognizable. Gone are her joyful declarations concerning the wondrous generosity of God. In their place we find a merciless demand regarding Abraham's first son, Ishmael. Sarah is determined that Isaac will never share his inheritance with his older brother.

Consequently, Ishmael and his mother, Hagar, are sent into the desert, meager provisions in hand. Their survival is doubtful, their suffering guaranteed apart from divine intervention.

Sarah's behavior, however upsetting, is not particularly uncommon. If we are honest, most of us have had times in our lives in which we greedily clutched God's blessings to our chests, tightfisted in our determination that we would never lose them.

Sometimes, we, like Sarah, get overly attached to God's gifts. We forget that our security is not found in the provision itself, but in the One who provides it. When this happens, our fear makes us selfish and possessive, calloused toward the needs of others.

May God set us free from the fear of scarcity. May He make us fall in love with Him instead of the gifts He gives us. May we, trusting in His kindness and faithfulness, open our hearts and hands to a world in need.

her heart is changed

Prompt

Ask God to search your heart for any place the fear of scarcity has taken root.

Ask Him to guard your heart with His peace and make you generous.

Dig Deeper

Psalm 65:11
II Corinthians 9:6–8
Proverbs 28:5

DAY 5

Leah, the Unloved

Slowly, and with tremendous difficulty, Leah rose from her place on a low stool in her tent to make her way outside for a bit of fresh air. When she pulled the tent flap back, a breeze tugged at the damp tendrils of her hair where it clung to her temples. She sighed at the welcome relief from the heat before wincing as an early contraction rippled across her lower abdomen.

Her eyes scanned the yard until they found Reuben and Simeon chasing each other in play. God had granted her two sons, a blessing so rich that she had been certain she would finally receive a small measure of the love her husband, Jacob, so easily lavished on Rachel, her sister and his second wife. After all, Rachel had borne him no children at all. She was barren. Unfortunately, however, there seemed to be no end to her beautiful, charming sister's hold on their shared husband.

Leah turned her gaze away from her sons to where Jacob and Rachel stood in a quiet corner of the yard, his head bent close to hers. As they watched the sun dip toward the horizon, painting the sky in bright strokes of pink and gold, Jacob slipped an arm around his favored wife and pressed his lips against her temple.

Leah's heart wrenched with an all too familiar ache that was quickly displaced by another contraction, this one stronger.

If God were gracious, her sons would have a new brother by morning. Two sons would become three, then she was certain her husband would finally love her.

Leah labored throughout the night, her cries keeping the whole camp awake. Then, as the first rays of sunlight broke over the horizon, she brought her baby boy into the world. When the midwife placed him on her chest, she wept for joy and named him "Levi."

"Now at last my husband will become attached to me, because I have borne him three sons," she said.

Moments later, Leah watched expectantly as the midwife wrapped the newborn in swaddling clothes and placed him in Jacob's arms. When he smiled down at his new son, her heart stirred with hope.

Then, without a word to her, he took Levi out into the yard where the rest of the family and the servants waited to welcome the new son into the family. From inside her tent, Leah listened to the sounds of celebration and allowed her heart to cling a bit more firmly to hope.

Three sons . . . he will love me now.

But . . . he didn't.

The boys grew, and years slipped past as Leah remained banished to the borders of love, close enough to watch it unfold in abundance at Rachel's feet, but too far away for her to even feel its faintest tender touch. Occasionally, however, Jacob still made his way into her tent when night fell.

Once again, Leah conceived.

This time, however, was different. As months passed and her abdomen grew, she refused to allow hope a foothold. She was older now, and years of heartbreak and disappointment had made her wiser.

Jacob didn't love her when she gave birth to Reuben or Simeon. Even when she bore him a third son, Levi, his heart remained cold. She knew with a painful surety that the child she was now carrying, whether boy or girl, was powerless to make her husband love her.

Soon, the familiar ebb and flow of labor swept her away. Finally, one last push, one final cry, and the midwife placed a fourth son on her chest.

Leah pulled the screaming, red bundle closer and named him Judah, in praise of a God whose love for her was so vast and deep that He had never once looked away from her suffering. His was a love that drew near to her and filled her aching heart so completely that it finally found its rest.

"This time," she said, "I will praise the Lord."

Scripture Reading

Read the passage below for the scriptural account of how God blessed Leah when He saw that she was unloved.

Genesis 29:31–35 NIV

When the Lord saw that Leah was not loved, He enabled her to conceive, but Rachel remained childless. Leah became pregnant and gave birth to a son. She named him Reuben, for she said, "It is because the Lord has seen my misery. Surely my husband will love me now."

She conceived again, and when she gave birth to a son she said, "Because the Lord heard that I am not loved, He gave me this one too." So she named him Simeon.

Again she conceived, and when she gave birth to a son she said, "Now at last my husband will become attached to me, because I have borne him three sons." So he was named Levi.

She conceived again, and when she gave birth to a son she said, "This time I will praise the Lord." So she named him Judah. Then she stopped having children.

Let's Review

In Leah's time, the greatest blessing a woman could bring to her husband was to bear him sons, so it makes sense that she hoped to earn Jacob's love in this way. What dangers lie in trying to "earn" another sinful human being's love?

The first line of our Scripture reading says, "The Lord saw that Leah was not loved. . . ." How does it make you feel to realize that Leah's broken heart mattered to God?

In the final verses of our Scripture reading, Leah finds a love upon which she can depend: God's. Why can we depend on the love of God when human love leaves us wanting?

Application

Loving another human being is risky business. Even the most well-intentioned among us will eventually let down someone whom we love. Human beings drop the ball even on their good days and are blatantly selfish and hurtful on their worst.

When we consider the harsh world through which our tender hearts must travel, it is very tempting to hide behind our tallest, strongest walls to avoid the perils of a broken heart.

If only that worked! But . . . it doesn't.

Because there is no love apart from vulnerability.

What is a fragile heart supposed to do? Where do we turn when love lets us down?

Leah hoped with the birth of each of her first three sons that she would earn her husband's love only to face the cruel reality that he still preferred her sister, Rachel. Then, with the birth of her fourth child, we see her focus shift. She is no longer striving to win her husband's heart. Instead, she is resting in the love that was hers all along—God's.

What about you? Is there an ache in your heart today for a love that will never leave you? It is already yours, friend. It has been all along. Rest today in the infinite, ever-abundant love of God.

Prompt

Write a prayer to God asking Him to heal the wounded places in your heart and to fill it with His love.

Dig Deeper

Psalm 36:5
Isaiah 54:10
Lamentations 3:22

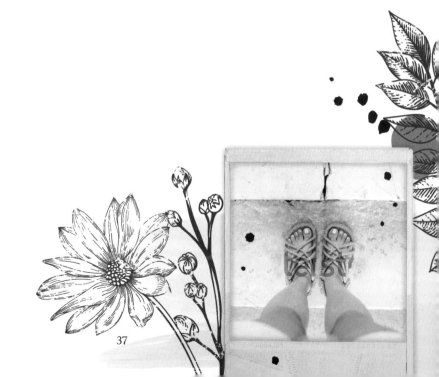

DAY 6

Rebekah, the Schemer

It all began with the tiniest, most worrisome idea.

What if her precious son, Jacob, didn't have all he needed? What if his future wasn't secure?

Fear dropped like a poisonous seed into Rebekah's heart and lodged there, growing quickly until it choked out all that was noble and good. It wrapped its thorny tendrils around love, honesty, and respect and squeezed tight until only fear remained.

Rebekah spent hours rolling the problem around in her head, obsessively turning it this way and that, searching for a solution until she thought of little else.

Perhaps this is what drove her to eavesdrop near the entrance to the tent where her blind and bedridden husband was talking to the oldest of the twins, Esau. After all, how could she ensure Jacob had the future he deserved if she didn't know what she was up against?

Rebekah held her breath and leaned a bit closer to better hear their conversation. Isaac was preparing to die and wanted to give Jacob's twin brother, Esau, his blessing before he passed away, but he wanted a little something first. Esau was a hunter, and Isaac had a craving for game cooked just the way he liked it.

This was the opportunity for which she had been waiting, but she needed to move quickly.

"Look," she said to Jacob, "I overheard your father say to your brother Esau, 'Bring me some game and prepare me some tasty food to eat, so that I may give you my blessing in the presence of the Lord before I die.' Now, my son, listen carefully and do what I tell you: Go out to the flock and bring me two choice young goats, so I can prepare some tasty food for your father, just the way he likes it. Then take it to your father to eat, so that he may give you his blessing before he dies."

But Jacob was hesitant. His father might be blind, but he wasn't senseless.

"But my brother Esau is a hairy man while I have smooth skin," he protested to his mother. "What if my father touches me? I would appear to be tricking him and would bring down a curse on myself rather than a blessing."

But Rebekah wasn't swayed. She was determined to elevate Jacob's position no matter the cost. "My son," she said, "let the curse fall on me. Just do what I say; go and get them for me."

While the goats were cooking, Rebekah found some of Esau's clothing and gave it to Jacob to wear so that he would smell like his brother. Then, she put goat skin on his arms and the backs of his hands, transforming his smooth skin into that which felt more like hairy Esau.

And the ruse worked! Isaac gave Esau's blessing to Jacob. The younger twin slipped out of the tent and out of sight just as his brother returned from the woods. A little while later, Esau carefully carried the meal he had prepared into his father's tent.

Rebekah stood just out of sight, waiting to see what would happen next.

It didn't take long for Isaac and Esau to realize they had been tricked. Esau's pitiful, anguished cry echoed throughout the camp. Soon, his grief turned to anger. He determined to ease his loss through revenge.

Later that evening, Rebekah hurriedly packed provisions for Jacob and sent him away for his own safety, intending to send word to him when it was safe for him to return.

But that day never came.

The price of her deceit and manipulation was so much higher than she could have ever imagined.

Scripture Reading

Read the passage below for the account of how Rebekah schemed to help Jacob steal his brother's blessing.

Genesis 27:1–13, 41–45 NIV

When Isaac was old and his eyes were so weak that he could no longer see, he called for Esau his older son and said to him, "My son."

"Here I am," he answered.

Isaac said, "I am now an old man and don't know the day of my death. Now then, get your equipment—your quiver and bow—and go out to the open country to hunt some wild game for me. Prepare me the kind of tasty food I like and bring it to me to eat, so that I may give you my blessing before I die."

Now Rebekah was listening as Isaac spoke to his son Esau. When Esau left for the open country to hunt game and bring it back, Rebekah said to her son Jacob, "Look, I overheard your father say to your brother Esau, 'Bring me some game and prepare me some tasty food to eat, so that I may give you my blessing in the presence of the Lord before I die.' Now, my son, listen carefully and do what I tell you: Go out to the flock and bring me two choice young goats, so I can prepare some tasty food for your father, just the way he likes it. Then take it to your father to eat, so that he may give you his blessing before he dies."

Jacob said to Rebekah his mother, "But my brother Esau is a hairy man while I have smooth skin. What if my father touches me? I would appear to be tricking him and would bring down a curse on myself rather than a blessing."

His mother said to him, "My son, let the curse fall on me. Just do what I say; go and get them for me."

***

Esau held a grudge against Jacob because of the blessing his father had given him. He said to himself, "The days of mourning for my father are near; then I will kill my brother Jacob."

When Rebekah was told what her older son Esau had said, she sent for her younger son Jacob and said to him, "Your brother Esau is planning to avenge himself by killing you. Now then, my son, do what I say: Flee at once to my brother Laban in Harran. Stay with him for a while until your brother's fury subsides. When your brother is no longer angry with you and forgets what you did to him, I'll send word for you to come back from there. Why should I lose both of you in one day?"

Let's Review

What dangers are inherent when a parent resorts to deceit and manipulation to help a child "get ahead?"

Re-read the Scripture account carefully. List all the consequences of Rebekah's scheming.

Sometimes, we attempt to exert control over a situation because we are afraid there "won't be enough to go around." What spiritual practices could you put in place to remind you to trust God to meet both your needs and those of the people you love?

Application

Rebekah wanted to secure Isaac's blessing for Jacob, but is it ever truly possible to bring about blessing through manipulation and deceit?

This is a question worth seriously pondering for each of us, but especially for the mothers among us. It is notoriously easy for moms to get tunnel vision when it comes to their kids' well-being, and the consequences can be far-reaching and disastrous.

Rebekah's intervention on Jacob's behalf came at a great cost to everyone involved. She harmed her aging, vulnerable husband by scheming to deceive him. She deeply wounded her older son, Esau, by helping his younger brother steal his blessing. Additionally, the already strained relationship between the two brothers was fractured to the point of Esau determining to murder Jacob in revenge.

Perhaps one of the most tragically ironic repercussions for Rebekah is that her actions necessitated her sending Jacob away from home to save his life, and as far as we can tell, she never saw her beloved son ever again.

Let Rebekah's mistakes be a lesson to all of us: we cause great harm to ourselves and others when we resort to manipulation in our attempt to inappropriately exert control over our circumstances.

We can trust God with our own well-being and with that of those we love. He is faithful, loving, and good.

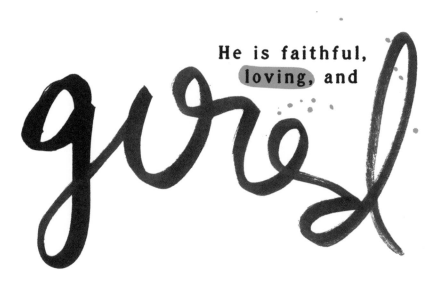

He is faithful, loving, and good

Prompt

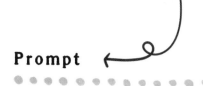

What fear in your life tempts you toward manipulation and control?

Take it to God in prayer.

Dig Deeper

Proverbs 22:8
Psalm 64
Proverbs 12:5

DAY 7

Jochebed, Mother of Moses

For nine precious months, Jochebed sheltered and nourished her son in her womb. There in the dark, he developed and grew, rocked to sleep by the steady rhythm of her heartbeat.

For three more months after his birth, she risked her own life to save his. Pharaoh had ordered that all Israelite baby boys be thrown to their deaths in the Nile River and so, Jochebed hid her son.

But then, the day came when he grew too big, his cry too strong, to hide him any longer.

Wrapped in a sling across her chest, the chubby cheeked baby smiled and cooed at her as she fought to hold back tears. Under the watchful eye of her older daughter, Miriam, Jochebed placed a basket on the table and sealed it tight with pitch, a waterproof glue-type substance.

When the pitch was dry, she nursed her baby one last time, wrapped him in blankets, and placed him in the ark. With his stomach full and the warmth of his mother still clinging to him, the baby boy drifted off to sleep.

Jochebed took a deep breath and closed her eyes for a moment to gather her strength. Then, she tucked the basket, and her baby, under her arm and began the short walk to the Nile. Once there, she parted the reeds and slipped the pitch-lined basket holding her baby boy out onto the water.

A tiny ark to hold her precious son . . .

It was a fragile hope, but the only one she had left to offer him. She had given him all she could. Now, all that was left was to whisper a prayer and . . . surrender him.

The rest was up to God.

Scripture Reading

Read the scriptural account below of Jochebed's heart-wrenching surrender of her son, Moses.

Exodus 1:22–2:10 NIV

Then Pharaoh gave this order to all his people: "Every Hebrew boy that is born you must throw into the Nile, but let every girl live."

Now a man of the tribe of Levi married a Levite woman, and she became pregnant and gave birth to a son. When she saw that he was a fine child, she hid him for three months. But when she could hide him no longer, she got a papyrus basket for him and coated it with tar and pitch. Then she placed the child in it and put it among the reeds along the bank of the Nile. His sister stood at a distance to see what would happen to him.

Then Pharaoh's daughter went down to the Nile to bathe, and her attendants were walking along the riverbank. She saw the basket among the reeds and sent her female slave to get it. She opened it and saw the baby. He was crying, and she felt sorry for him. "This is one of the Hebrew babies," she said.

Then his sister asked Pharaoh's daughter, "Shall I go and get one of the Hebrew women to nurse the baby for you?"

"Yes, go," she answered. So the girl went and got the baby's mother. Pharaoh's daughter said to her, "Take this baby and nurse him for me, and I will pay you." So the woman took the baby and nursed him. When the child grew older, she took him to Pharaoh's daughter and he became her son. She named him Moses, saying, "I drew him out of the water."

Let's Review

Imagine you are Jochebed, and you have just realized that you are expecting a baby. Describe what you are thinking and feeling.

Women will go to great lengths to protect those they love, but like Jochebed, we all reach our limit at some point. What brings you peace in these moments?

Our Scripture reading tells us that not only did God save Moses' life, He returned the baby to his mother until he was weaned. Imagine the moment Pharaoh's daughter placed Moses back in his mother's arms. What might Jochebed have been thinking and feeling?

Application

Genesis 7 tells us the harrowing story of a worldwide flood sent by God as a creational reset of sorts because humanity had slipped into such depths of violence and bloodshed that a do-over seemed the only option.

But . . . God preserved a remnant. One man, Noah, was still attentive to God's leading, so God instructed Noah to build an ark for the preservation of his family as well as two of every kind of animal.

Exodus chapter two tells us of another ark, this much smaller one fashioned by a grieving mother's hands to give her baby boy the only chance she could afford him when all her other resources came up short. With this ark, God saved the baby boy, Moses, who then grew up to save and lead his people to freedom from Egyptian slavery.

Most of us know a "mama bear" who has done amazing things for the love of a child. Jochebed was certainly one of these. She courageously hid her baby for as long as she could, and when the moment came in which she was no longer able to do so, she gave him the only gift she had left to give: she tucked him into a pitch-sealed basket and set him afloat on the Nile.

Jochebed's lesson for us is a simple one, but far from easy:

When we have done all we can to protect and provide for those we love who are in crisis, we must surrender them into the loving care of God.

Letting go is hard, isn't it?

It feels like quitting. It feels like failure. *It just feels . . . wrong.*

But there are moments when letting go is both our only choice and the *best choice* because in doing so, we make room for God to move in unexpected, miraculous ways.

Are you heartbroken over a loved one in crisis? Remember that God loves them far more than you could ever imagine and that while your human resources are limited, His are infinite.

Our loving, rescuing God is mighty to save.

God is *mighty*

Prompt

Write a prayer asking God to help you surrender those you love into His faithful care.

Dig Deeper

Matthew 10:29–30
Psalm 18:16–17
Isaiah 43:1–7

DAY 8

Miriam, the Complainer

Miriam huddled outside the camp—alone, sick, and filled with shame. She lifted the sleeve of her robe and was filled with fresh horror at the sight of her skin, scaly and white as snow.

The irony of God's punishment for her complaining against Moses was not lost on her. She had resented his taking of a dark-skinned wife, and so God inflicted her with a skin disease that robbed her own skin of all color before banishing her outside the borders of the camp for seven days.

How had she, a prophetess of Israel and sister of Moses, fallen so far?

On the edge of the camp, with nothing to do but think, her resentful, slanderous complaints concerning Moses haunted her. She remembered how haughtily she had protested his marriage and his position as leader.

"Has the LORD spoken only through Moses? Hasn't He also spoken through us?" she complained to her brother, Aaron.

She felt so sure of her position, so indignant and superior right up until the moment when she was called before almighty God. God descended around her, Moses, and Aaron in the pillar of cloud and gave voice to His fury. He had heard her slander and complaining, and His message to her was clear: while He might speak through her and other prophets, Moses was the one true leader of Israel. Only Moses spoke with God "face to face" (Exodus 33:11).

Then the cloud lifted, and she saw Moses' and Aaron's eyes grow wide with terror as they looked at her. Aaron turned to Moses and began to plead with him to speak to God on her behalf. He did, and God would grant her healing, but not before He gave her seven long days to think about her actions.

Miriam shook her head in dismay. She had been a fool; she had forgotten that to hear the voice of God and speak on His behalf was a privilege. The only response to such a gift was gratitude.

Soon, God would restore Miriam to her brothers and the rest of Israel, her skin made new.

And with a heart set right—grateful and humble, once again.

Scripture Reading

Read the Scripture passage below for the account of how Miriam succumbed to a spirit of complaining.

Numbers 12:1–15 NIV

Miriam and Aaron began to talk against Moses because of his Cushite wife, for he had married a Cushite. "Has the Lord spoken only through Moses?" they asked. "Hasn't He also spoken through us?" And the Lord heard this.

(Now Moses was a very humble man, more humble than anyone else on the face of the earth.)

At once the Lord said to Moses, Aaron and Miriam, "Come out to the tent of meeting, all three of you." So the three of them went out. Then the Lord came down in a pillar of cloud; He stood at the entrance to the tent and summoned Aaron and Miriam. When the two of them stepped forward, He said, "Listen to my words:

"When there is a prophet among you,
　I, the Lord, reveal Myself to them in visions,
　I speak to them in dreams.
But this is not true of my servant Moses;
　he is faithful in all My house.
With him I speak face to face,
　clearly and not in riddles;
　he sees the form of the Lord.
Why then were you not afraid
　to speak against my servant Moses?"

The anger of the Lord burned against them, and He left them.

When the cloud lifted from above the tent, Miriam's skin was leprous—it became as white as snow. Aaron turned toward her and saw that she had a defiling skin disease, and he said to Moses, "Please, my lord, I ask you not to hold against us the sin we have so foolishly committed. Do not let her be like a stillborn infant coming from its mother's womb with its flesh half eaten away."

So Moses cried out to the Lord, "Please, God, heal her!"

The Lord replied to Moses, "If her father had spit in her face, would she not have been in disgrace for seven days? Confine her outside the camp for seven days; after that she can be brought back." So Miriam was confined outside the camp for seven days, and the people did not move on till she was brought back.

Let's Review

Today's story illustrates the destructive power of a complaining spirit that spread through Israel like a disease until it infected Moses's own brother and sister. Have you ever witnessed a situation in which complaining seemed "contagious"? What were the consequences?

A complaining spirit often is rooted in ingratitude. What steps can you take to remain grateful, even in hard times?

It seems that Miriam was punished more severely than Aaron because she was doing the lion's share of complaining, and that he was complicit by his silence. How does it make you feel to realize that we can commit harm not only by what we say but also by keeping silent in the face of sin?

Application

It is sobering to realize that our complaining spirit is both destructive and contagious. Once one person begins to voice their grievances, resentment and anger spread like wildfire whether it be within a family, church, or even a country.

Take a moment sometime to listen—really listen—to the cable news station of your choice, consciously noting any statements of negativity, resentment, or slander. If you really want to go down that rabbit hole, do the same thing for social media.

It is shocking how saturated our national discourse has become with ingratitude and complaining.

In Numbers 11 and 12, we watch this same phenomenon unfold in the tribes of Israel. They complain about the food God provides, saying that they had better food as slaves in Egypt (forgetting that they were SLAVES). They complain and complain and complain until Moses begs God to kill him so that he won't have to deal with them anymore (Numbers 11:15). Eventually, this complaining spirit makes its way to Moses' inner circle, infecting his own sister and brother.

Let Miriam's story be a warning to us all today. May we practice relentless, intentional gratitude to guard our hearts against resentment.

and with a heart set right—grateful & humble

Prompt

Have you fallen into a spirit of complaining? Ask God to forgive you and to give you a grateful heart.

Dig Deeper

Romans 12:3–21
I Corinthians 12:1–11
Philippians 2:12–18

DAY 9

Rahab, the Restored

Rahab stood at the base of the stairs leading to her roof, her heart pounding in her chest. Each of the afternoon's series of tense events had led her to this moment when she would leverage everything to save her and her family's lives.

Not long after the foreigners (spies from Israel) arrived at her door, the sound of Jericho's soldiers rang through the streets as they began searching for the men. In that moment, Rahab made a quick calculation of how best to survive. Most people, she knew, would have surrendered the men to the soldiers to face torture and certain death. Instead, Rahab betrayed her own people by keeping the spies hidden.

When the soldiers pounded on her door, demanding she bring the men out to them, she lied. She told them that although the men had been there, they had already left. Then, she craftily pointed the search party in the wrong direction and sent them on their way.

It was a high-stakes gamble, and the lives of her and her family were the currency.

Rahab willed her racing heart to still and placed one hand on the exterior wall of her home, which was also the exterior wall of the city. She lived in the cheapest rent district of Jericho, right in the casemate wall* that surrounded the city. When under the threat of siege (if the city had the time to do so) the city could fill space between the double walls with rubble, rendering the wall infinitely stronger than the exterior wall alone. Otherwise, poor people like Rahab lived there.

The rent was cheap because if Jericho was attacked and the gate breached, those living in the walls were destined to be the first to die.

Rahab took another deep breath and then made her way up the stairs to bargain for her life. When she stepped onto the roof, she was met by the wary gaze of the two strangers. Then, her voice trembling, she began to plead her case.

"I know that the Lord has given you this land and that a great fear of you has fallen on us, so that all who live in this country are melting in fear because of you. We have heard how the Lord dried up the water of the Red Sea for you when you came out of Egypt, and what you did to Sihon and Og, the two kings of the Amorites east of the Jordan, whom you completely destroyed. When we heard of it, our hearts melted in fear and everyone's courage failed because of you, for the Lord your God is God in heaven above and on the earth below.

"Now then, please swear to me by the Lord that you will show kindness to my family, because I have shown kindness to you. Give me a sure sign that you will spare the lives of my father and mother, my brothers and sisters, and all who belong to them—and that you will save us from death."

The men immediately agreed to her proposal, asking only that she keep their location secret and that she bring all of her family into the safety of her home before the siege. They instructed her to tie a scarlet cord in her window, a signal to Israel's armies to spare her and her family.

Moments later, Rahab watched the men disappear into the night as she let them down through a window in the wall with a rope. When she felt the rope go slack, she quickly pulled it back inside and tied a scarlet cord in its place. For a moment, she held the cord between her fingers, a fragile tether between her family and survival . . .

A tangible symbol of her hope for her future, a life better than the scramble for survival that was all she had ever known.

Scripture Reading

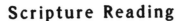

Read the passage below for the account of Rahab's brave decision to hide Israel's spies.

Joshua 2:1–21 NIV

Then Joshua son of Nun secretly sent two spies from Shittim. "Go, look over the land," he said, "especially Jericho." So they went and entered the house of a prostitute named Rahab and stayed there.

The king of Jericho was told, "Look, some of the Israelites have come here tonight to spy out the land." So the king of Jericho sent this message to Rahab: "Bring out the men who came to you and entered your house, because they have come to spy out the whole land."

But the woman had taken the two men and hidden them. She said, "Yes, the men came to me, but I did not know where they had come from. At dusk, when it was time to close the city gate, they left. I don't know which way they went. Go after them quickly. You may catch up with them." (But she had taken them up to the roof and hidden them under the stalks of flax she had laid out on the roof.) So the men set out in pursuit of the spies on the road that leads to the fords of the Jordan . . .

Before the spies lay down for the night, she went up on the roof and said to them, "I know that the Lord has given you this land and that a great fear of you has fallen on us, so that all who live in this country are melting in fear because of you. We have heard how the Lord dried up the water of the Red Sea for you when you came out of Egypt, and what you did to Sihon and Og, the two kings of the Amorites east of the Jordan, whom you completely destroyed. When we heard of it, our hearts melted in fear and everyone's courage failed because of you, for the Lord your God is God in heaven above and on the earth below.

"Now then, please swear to me by the Lord that you will show kindness to my family, because I have shown kindness to you. Give me a sure sign that you will spare the lives of my father and mother, my brothers and sisters, and all who belong to them—and that you will save us from death."

"Our lives for your lives!" the men assured her. "If you don't tell what we are doing, we will treat you kindly and faithfully when the Lord gives us the land."

So she let them down by a rope through the window, for the house she lived in was part of the city wall. She said to them, "Go to the hills so the pursuers will not find you. Hide yourselves there three days until they return, and then go on your way."

Now the men had said to her, "This oath you made us swear will not be binding on us unless, when we enter the land, you have tied this scarlet cord in the window through which you let us down, and unless you have brought your father and mother, your brothers and all your family into your house . . .

"Agreed," she replied. "Let it be as you say." So she sent them away, and they departed. And she tied the scarlet cord in the window.

Let's Review

When you read today's Scripture, were you surprised that God would use a prostitute to save His people? Why or why not?

Psalm 106 reflects on God's parting of the Red Sea, saying that God saved His people for His name's sake. How does Rahab's rooftop proposal to the spies show that God's name had been "made famous" because of His mighty works on Israel's behalf?

Rahab's story shows us that God's purpose for our lives is not limited by the mistakes we have made. Most of us tend to beat ourselves up to some degree for the moments in which we were our "worst selves." How does God's mercy in Rahab's life challenge you to hold those moments in greater grace?

Application

It is a rare woman who willingly chooses prostitution as a career path. It is far more likely that Rahab turned to prostitution out of desperation to survive. Rahab had most likely wrestled with scarcity her entire life. She was accustomed to quickly appraising a situation and coming to a decision about which path would grant her the best chance of living to see another day.

It is easy to imagine her doing this when she opened her door to find two foreign spies standing on her threshold. In her speech to the two men, she tells them why she decided to hide them instead of turning them over to Jericho's soldiers: she had heard about the mighty works of God on Israel's behalf and had concluded that the Almighty could not be beaten.

Even more striking is her final declaration that Israel's God was "God in heaven above and on the earth below" (Joshua 2:11 NIV). There is little doubt that Rahab had grown up worshipping several "gods." That she, a prostitute, is found declaring the omnipotence of Israel's "one true God" is both astounding . . . and humbling.

We are so quick to dismiss those we deem more sinful than we are. We place limits on the grace of God. We don't want to believe there is redemption for certain people because their actions have put them beyond a clean slate and a purpose. The inclusion of Rahab's story in Scripture refutes this notion, daring us to believe that His grace is as deep as the sea, His mercy as high as the heavens.

But God isn't finished teaching us a few things about grace through Rahab's life. We find her mentioned again in the first chapter of Matthew in a "Where are they now?" sort of moment. We are delighted to find in Matthew 1:5 that God drives the point of His limitless redemption home by including Rahab's name in the genealogy of the Messiah.

Rahab, the prostitute, became the great-great grandmother of Israel's greatest king, King David, and the ancestor of Jesus the Messiah.

Is there some sin in your past that haunts you, causing you to doubt the hope of your future? God's inclusion of Rahab's story in Scripture assures us that His arm is never too short to save. His grace is enough.

God in heaven above & on earth below

Prompt

Write a prayer asking God to help you leave your most painful failings in His loving hands. Ask Him to help you trust in His mercy that never fails.

Dig Deeper

Matthew 21:31–32
Isaiah 57:18–19
Psalm 51:7

DAY 10

Deborah and Jael, Women of War

Deborah stood on the slopes of Mount Tabor gazing out at the valley below. A vast army, powerfully equipped with war chariots, was slowly filling the space. Even from a distance, she could see their swords, shields, and spears flashing in the sunlight as warhorses, ready for battle, impatiently pawed at the verdant grass beneath their hooves.

Barak, leader of the armies of Israel stood with her, his face grim. Behind her, the 10,000 who had answered her call to war were virtually weaponless, stripped bare of all means of defending themselves during Jabin's twenty-year oppression of them.

Now, his fierce general, Sisera, was prepared to annihilate them.

Suddenly, a strong breeze rose, driving heavy storm clouds before it. With terrifying suddenness, the bright day turned dark. Lighting flashed, thunder roared, and the skies broke open, unleashing a blinding rain on the valley below.

Deborah smiled. God had joined the battle.

She held her hand aloft, signaling to the men to remain still until she gave them the order to engage the enemy. Far beneath them, horses screamed in terror as the sky raged. Then, a louder, deeper roar rose above the fury. Deborah turned toward the sound to find that the peaceful Kishon River had transformed into a monster, thirsty for prey. A wall of water rushed into the valley, sweeping chariots into the flood and burying their wheels deep in the mud.

It was time. Deborah dropped her hand, and her soldiers raised a deafening war cry as they rushed down the mountainside. God was setting His people free.

Sisera leapt from his destroyed chariot and fled for his life. He ran north, hoping to make it to his home in Hazor before the Israelite army overtook him. At last, weak with exhaustion, he drew near the tent of Heber the Kenite and was met by Heber's wife, Jael.

"Come, my lord, come right in," she said. "Don't be afraid."

Gratefully, Sisera ducked into the tent before collapsing onto the floor. Jael gently tucked a blanket around him before ducking outside to get some milk for him to drink. She placed the bowl in his hands, and watched as he drained it.

Then, he handed the empty bowl back to her before once again collapsing onto the tent floor and falling fast asleep.

Quietly, Jael crept from the tent. Once outside, she glanced around for something she might use as a weapon. Her eyes rested on a tent stake and the mallet she used to drive it into the ground.

With grim determination, she picked up the heavy stake, the iron rough against her left palm before grasping the wooden handle of the mallet in her right.

Silently, she pushed the tent flap aside and stepped into the dim interior toward her prey.

Scripture Reading

Read the passage below to discover how God used two women to deliver Israel from its oppressors during a time of war.

Judges 4:1–9, 14–24 NIV

Again the Israelites did evil in the eyes of the Lord, now that Ehud was dead. So the Lord sold them into the hands of Jabin king of Canaan, who reigned in Hazor. Sisera, the commander of his army, was based in Harosheth Haggoyim. Because he had nine hundred chariots fitted with iron and had cruelly oppressed the Israelites for twenty years, they cried to the Lord for help.

Now Deborah, a prophet, the wife of Lappidoth, was leading Israel at that time. She held court under the Palm of Deborah between Ramah and Bethel in the hill country of Ephraim, and the Israelites went up to her to have their disputes decided. She sent for Barak son of Abinoam from Kedesh in Naphtali and said to him, "The Lord, the God of Israel, commands you: 'Go, take with you ten thousand men of Naphtali and Zebulun and lead them up to Mount Tabor. I will lead Sisera, the commander of Jabin's army, with his chariots and his troops to the Kishon River and give him into your hands.'"

Barak said, "If you go with me, I will go; but if you don't go with me, I won't go."

"Certainly I will go with you," said Deborah. "But because of the course you are taking, the honor will not be yours, for the Lord will deliver Sisera into the hands of a woman." . . .

***

Then Deborah said to Barak, "Go! This is the day the Lord has given Sisera into your hands. Has not the Lord gone ahead of you?" . . .

Barak pursued the chariots and army as far as Harosheth Haggoyim, and all Sisera's troops fell by the sword; not a man was left. Sisera, meanwhile, fled on foot to the tent of Jael, the wife of Heber the Kenite, because there was an alliance between Jabin king of Hazor and the family of Heber the Kenite.

Jael went out to meet Sisera and said to him, "Come, my lord, come right in. Don't be afraid." So he entered her tent, and she covered him with a blanket.

"I'm thirsty," he said. "Please give me some water." She opened a skin of milk, gave him a drink, and covered him up.

"Stand in the doorway of the tent," he told her. "If someone comes by and asks you, 'Is anyone in there?' say 'No.'"

But Jael, Heber's wife, picked up a tent peg and a hammer and went quietly to him while he lay fast asleep, exhausted. She drove the peg through his temple into the ground, and he died.

Just then Barak came by in pursuit of Sisera, and Jael went out to meet him. "Come," she said, "I will show you the man you're looking for." So he went in with her, and there lay Sisera with the tent peg through his temple—dead.

Let's Review

Deborah was a prophet, a judicial leader who decided disputes among the men and women of Israel, and a fierce military leader. Do any of these roles catch you by surprise? If so, which ones and why?

Barak hesitated to go into battle, but not Deborah. What do you think was the source of her fierce courage?

Jael gave the exhausted Sisera milk to drink, tucked him in for a nap, and then drove a tent stake through his temple. Are you surprised to find this "warrior woman's" story included in Scripture? Why or why not?

Application

"Then the Israelites did what was evil in the sight of the Lord and served the Baals, and they abandoned the Lord, the God of their ancestors" (Judges 2:11–12 NRSVA).

This verse, found in Judges 2, summarizes for us the "why" of the book of Judges. After Joshua's death, Israel did not remain faithful to God for very long, falling into a three hundred-year period of time in which she "abandoned God" over and over again, prompting Him to remove His cover of protection over her.

Each time this cycle repeated, and Israel found herself suffering under the boot of the nations surrounding her, she cried out to God for deliverance. Judges 2:18 (NRSVA) tells us that "the Lord would be moved to pity by their groaning because of those who persecuted and oppressed them," prompting Him to send His people "judges" to deliver them.

According to Robert Alter, author of *The Hebrew Bible*, the word traditionally translated "judge" is "*shofet*." This word has two meanings, one implying a judicial role and the other "leader" or "chieftain." It is this second meaning that is relevant in the book of Judges (although Deborah, the subject of our study today, also filled a judicial role).

A "judge" in Israel was a military leader raised up and empowered by God to rescue His people from their oppressors. Deborah was all about breaking out of the traditional roles afforded to her as a woman in ancient Israel.

- She was a prophet, serving as God's mouthpiece to His people.
- Deborah also held a judicial role, hearing cases underneath a palm tree that bore her name.
- Finally, she fulfilled the role of military leader for Israel, accompanying Barak into battle when he refused to go without her.

Theologian Alfred Edersheim makes the fascinating observation that her designation "wife of Lappidoth" (Judges 4:4) is more accurately translated "woman of a torch-like spirit."

Deborah was undeniably fierce, as was her Kenite counterpart, Jael.

The Kenites were an Arab tribe who lived among the Israelites. Jael was their "Deborah." When Sisera, on the run from the Israelites, winds up in front of her tent, she lures him inside with the promise of safety and hospitality only to drive a tent peg through his temple while he sleeps. When Barak finally shows up, there is little left for him to do. The final battle had already been decidedly won—by a woman.

Deborah and Jael's stories challenge us to recognize that God uses women in nontraditional roles to advance His kingdom. God is God. He is going to do things how He wants and when He wants. He is not limited by our narrow ideas of purpose; therefore, we must stay close to Him, listening for His leading.

Prompt

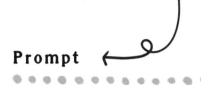

Ask God to open your eyes and heart to His purpose for your life, enabling you by His Spirit to respond with an obedient heart however He may lead.

Dig Deeper

Deborah's Song
Judges 5:1–9
Judges 5:10–27
Judges 5:28–31

DAY 11

Naomi

How many steps were there between Moab and Bethlehem, between "The Land of Empty" and "The House of Bread"?

One step out the front door. Five hundred more to the edge of town. A couple of thousand down the mountainside, and a few thousand more to the other side of the Dead Sea. More steps still until fields of grain, dancing in the breeze, finally welcomed Naomi home.

Step by step, Naomi walked away from the country of her sojourning and back home again. Grief, and her daughter-in-law, Ruth, were her traveling companions.

Empty... Empty... Empty...

Each footfall, whether upon sand, rock, or salty shore, seemed to echo the same refrain. Ten years had passed since Naomi first walked this path. Back then, she and her young family were fleeing another kind of emptiness. A famine in Bethlehem had left fields and pantries barren, so she, her husband, and two sons left home for the lush plains of Moab.

There, they found plentiful grain . . . and a new life. In Moab, Naomi's sons grew from boys into young men. Once they married, everyone, including Naomi, expected babies would soon follow.

But in three brutal strokes, it was all taken from her. First, her husband died. Next, a son. Then, unfathomably, his brother followed him to the grave.

From deep in the midnight of mourning, Naomi took a good look around her and decided it was time to go back home.

Thousands of steps later, Naomi and Ruth neared Bethlehem, the breadbasket of Israel. When they arrived on the outskirts of town, they found the fields of barley overflowing with harvesters and grain.

Women she had not seen for years stopped in their labors to gasp in astonishment at her return.

"Can this be Naomi?" they asked each other.

Naomi, whose name meant "pleasant," couldn't bear it.

"Don't call me Naomi," she told them. "Call me Mara [which means "bitter"] because the Almighty has made my life very bitter. I went away full, but the LORD has brought me back empty."

It all seemed so final in that moment. The curtain of loss and grief, impenetrable.

But no wasteland of loss, no matter how vast, is any match for the God of abundance.

At the end of the book of Ruth, we find Naomi *restored*. Her daughter-in-law Ruth has married a wealthy and honorable landowner, Boaz, and Naomi has taken her place as honored family matriarch.

God, however, wasn't finished. He was still writing the end of Naomi's story of abundance. Reading the final verses of Ruth is like watching a miracle unfold.

Ruth gives birth to a baby boy . . .

Naomi takes the child in her arms . . .

Her friends, who know all too well how much she has lost, proclaim in awe, "Naomi has a son!"

Scripture Reading

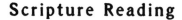

Read the Scripture excerpts from the book of Ruth to learn more about Naomi's heartbreak and how God brought new life to her when she least expected it.

Ruth 1:1–5, 19–22, 4:13–17 NIV

In the days when the judges ruled, there was a famine in the land. So a man from Bethlehem in Judah, together with his wife and two sons, went to live for a while in the country of Moab. The man's name was Elimelek, his wife's name was Naomi, and the names of his two sons were Mahlon and Kilion. They were Ephrathites from Bethlehem, Judah. And they went to Moab and lived there.

Now Elimelek, Naomi's husband, died, and she was left with her two sons. They married Moabite women, one named Orpah and the other Ruth. After they had lived there about ten years, both Mahlon and Kilion also died, and Naomi was left without her two sons and her husband.

***

So the two women went on until they came to Bethlehem. When they arrived in Bethlehem, the whole town was stirred because of them, and the women exclaimed, "Can this be Naomi?"

"Don't call me Naomi," she told them. "Call me Mara, because the Almighty has made my life very bitter. I went away full, but the Lord has brought me back empty. Why call me Naomi? The Lord has afflicted me; the Almighty has brought misfortune upon me."

So Naomi returned from Moab accompanied by Ruth the Moabite, her daughter-in-law, arriving in Bethlehem as the barley harvest was beginning.

***

So Boaz took Ruth and she became his wife. When he made love to her, the Lord enabled her to conceive, and she gave birth to a son. The women said to Naomi: "Praise be to the Lord, who this day has not left you without a guardian-redeemer. May he become famous throughout Israel! He will renew your life and sustain you in your old age. For your daughter-in-law, who loves you and who is better to you than seven sons, has given him birth."

Then Naomi took the child in her arms and cared for him. The women living there said, "Naomi has a son!" And they named him Obed. He was the father of Jesse, the father of David.

Let's Review

When Naomi and Ruth arrive in Bethlehem, Naomi tells the women who greet her to no longer call her Naomi but "Mara" which means "bitter." At this moment in her life, Naomi can imagine no possible future beyond the loss she has suffered. What are some ways we can offer each other comfort, kindness, and mercy in the moments when hope has been lost?

One of the predominant themes of the book of Ruth is the transition from emptiness to fullness. For example, when Naomi and her family left Bethlehem for Moab, they were fleeing famine to live in a land where food was plentiful. Think through today's reading. How many examples do you see of this theme? Jot them down below.

One of the most beautiful verses in today's reading is found in Ruth 4:15 which reads, "He will renew your life and sustain you in your old age." Where in your life do you find yourself longing for God's renewal and sustenance?

Application

Naomi's story is a beautiful snapshot of the theme of restoration that runs throughout Scripture. As she and her daughter-in-law, Ruth, make the journey from Moab to Bethlehem, Naomi's life seems cloaked in irreparable loss. She expresses the depths of her devastation when she says, "I went away full, but the Lord has brought me back empty" (Ruth 1:21 NIV).

At some point in our lives, most of us will face grief that is far beyond our ability to bear, a loss so profoundly painful that we lose sight of any hope for our future. This is not a personal failing or a sign that our faith is lacking. It is, simply, what it means to be human.

Naomi's story reminds us of this truth, but it also challenges us to suspend judgment concerning our future because it just might be that God still has another chapter to write in our life story.

Our God is ever on the move, leading us from loss to restoration, from emptiness to abundance, and from heartbreak to joy so that with the psalmist we might proclaim, "Weeping may linger for the night, but joy comes with the morning" (Psalm 30:5 NRSVA).

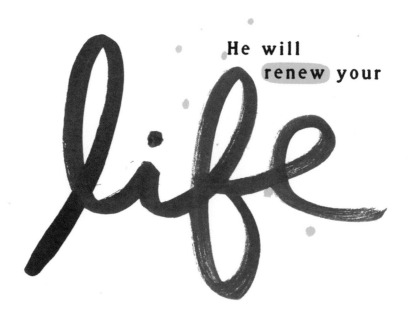

He will renew your life

Prompt

Have you ever been bitterly disappointed and left wondering why God would allow such heartbreak into your life? If so, journal about that experience below. If not, write a prayer asking God to help you trust Him when life inevitably turns out far differently than you have planned.

Dig Deeper

Psalm 51:12
Psalm 4:6–8
Psalm 30:4–5

DAY 12

Ruth

Ruth moved quickly and quietly through the darkened streets of Bethlehem. Lamplight flickered from the windows of nearby homes, casting uncertain shadows before her feet. Occasionally, the quiet was interrupted by the sound of laughter, the murmur of conversation, or the shuffling of animals as they bedded down for the night in their stables.

And the sound of her own heartbeat, deafening, throughout it all.

It would be dangerous for any young woman to be alone in the streets at night, but for Ruth, a foreigner, even more so. What is more, the mission ahead of her was scandalous at best, and potentially dangerous too. Everything depended on her stealth . . . and the kind of man Boaz was.

She was risking everything on the belief that Boaz was a man of honor and that he would use his position and power to protect her rather than take advantage of her.

A moment later, the deep voices of men enjoying their dinner and wine drifted to her from the threshing floor. Ruth drew near, clinging to the shadows, and waited for the lamplight to dim as the men settled down to sleep for the night. When all was quiet, she tiptoed to where Boaz lay sleeping, lay down at the end of his sleeping mat in the place of a servant, and pulled the blanket back from his feet.

It didn't take long for the chilly night air on his bare feet to rouse him.

"Who are you?" he demanded, shocked to find a woman on the threshing floor in the middle of the night.

"I am Ruth, your servant," she replied. "Spread the corner of your garment over me. . . ."

Corner of your garment . . . also translated, "under your wing."

It was the language of protection and covering, the language of both God's relationship with Israel and that of a husband and wife. In a world in which she was easy prey for a man, Ruth dared to ask Boaz to use his power to shelter her, to be a man whose heart reflected God's own.

And he was.

He instructed her to stay in his protection until morning, then he filled her shawl with provision and her heart with a promise: he would take the necessary legal steps to make her his wife and would do so without delay. He even protected her reputation, instructing his workers to tell no one that a woman came to the threshing floor at night.

Ruth could have had her pick of the young men in town, rich or poor. Instead, she chose a man whose character reflected God's heart for her.

Protective. Kind. Generous.
A promise keeper . . .

Boaz wasted no time going through all of the proper channels to make Ruth his wife, not only securing her present but also preserving her honor forever in the lineage of the Messiah.

> *Salmon the father of Boaz, whose mother was Rahab,*
> *Boaz the father of Obed, whose mother was Ruth,*
> *Obed the father of Jesse,*
> *and Jesse the father of King David (Matthew 1:5–6 NIV).*

King David, from whom descended a man named Joseph, who married a peasant girl named Mary, who gave birth to a baby boy and named Him Jesus, because He was born to save His people from their sins (Matthew 1:21).

Scripture Reading

Read the scriptural account of Ruth's nighttime visit to the threshing floor.

Ruth 3:6–17 NIV

So she went down to the threshing floor and did everything her mother-in-law told her to do.

When Boaz had finished eating and drinking and was in good spirits, he went over to lie down at the far end of the grain pile. Ruth approached quietly, uncovered his feet and lay down. In the middle of the night something startled the man; he turned—and there was a woman lying at his feet!

"Who are you?" he asked.

"I am your servant Ruth," she said. "Spread the corner of your garment over me, since you are a guardian-redeemer of our family."

"The Lord bless you, my daughter," he replied. "This kindness is greater than that which you showed earlier: You have not run after the younger men, whether rich or poor. And now, my daughter, don't be afraid. I will do for you all you ask. All the people of my town know that you are a woman of noble character. Although it is true that I am a guardian-redeemer of our family, there is another who is more closely related than I. Stay here for the night, and in the morning if he wants to do his duty as your guardian-redeemer, good; let him redeem you. But if he is not willing, as surely as the Lord lives I will do it. Lie here until morning."

So she lay at his feet until morning, but got up before anyone could be recognized; and he said, "No one must know that a woman came to the threshing floor."

He also said, "Bring me the shawl you are wearing and hold it out." When she did so, he poured into it six measures of barley and placed the bundle on her. Then he went back to town.

When Ruth came to her mother-in-law, Naomi asked, "How did it go, my daughter?"

Then she told her everything Boaz had done for her and added, "He gave me these six measures of barley, saying, 'Don't go back to your mother-in-law empty-handed.'"

Let's Review

Ruth's courageous nighttime journey to the threshing floor was a risky one. As a woman alone, she could easily have been attacked on the way to where Boaz was working with his men. Once there, Boaz might also have taken advantage of her. What part do you think courage plays in seeking out God's best for our lives?

When Ruth asks Boaz to become her kinsman redeemer *and marry her, she uses the beautiful phrase, "Spread the corner of your garment over me." (v. 9). This is reflective of both the marriage ceremony as well as language common in Scripture to describe God's tender care for His people. When you think of the kindness of God in that He "spreads His wing" over you in loving protection, how does that make you feel?*

Ruth was very beautiful and could have had her pick of any of the young men in town. In Boaz, she chose a man whose heart reflected the heart of God for her. Stop for a moment and consider the various relationships in your life—friendships, family, partnerships, your work, and worship community. Where have you made choices that reflect God's heart for you? Are there any relationships that are harmful to you?

Application

Ruth was a woman of godly expectations which were rooted in a deep understanding of her worth. Today's text makes it clear that she was extraordinarily beautiful, and as a result, could have had her pick of any of the handsome, young men working in the fields (Ruth 3:10). Instead, she chose Boaz, a man of honor who was worthy of her and whose treatment of her reflected God's heart for her.

Embracing Ruth's approach to life is not always easy for us. Sometimes, we get God's call to love and service confused with codependency. The truth, however, is that it is impossible to truly love and serve another if we have not first recognized our own worth as image bearers of God.

Let us never forget that God fashioned us with infinite love and imparted immutable dignity to us as His children. He treats us with the utmost protection, provision, and delight. Doesn't it stand to reason that He would want us to choose relationships that do the same?

under your wing

Prompt

Take the time to prayerfully journal about your worth as a child of God. Ask God to show you where in your life He longs for you to set godly standards for your relationships.

Dig Deeper

Psalm 17:8
Psalm 91:4
Luke 13:34

DAY 13

Bathsheba, Wife of Uriah

Slowly, carefully, Bathsheba folded her coarse mourning garments before gently laying them in the basket beneath the window. For a moment, her hand lingered on them.

How could she end her period of mourning for her husband when her heart was still so shattered?

She took a shuddering breath, wiped the tears from her cheeks, and closed the basket. Wearily, she lowered herself onto a low stool and gathered her undergarment into her lap along with a needle and thread. According to custom, she had torn it upon receiving news of her husband's death. Now that her official period of mourning was over, she would mend the garment.

But who would mend her heart?

As needle and thread passed through the fabric, slowly closing the two sides together, her mind wandered back to the night when everything began falling apart. She had gone onto the roof for a bath, unaware that King David was watching her from his palace. Instead of going to war he had remained at home, sending others, including her husband, Uriah, to battle in his stead.

When a servant knocked on her door later that evening, announcing that the king had ordered her to come to the palace, she had little choice but to obey. She carefully tucked a still damp strand of hair back beneath her head covering and followed him the short distance between her home and the palace gates.

Once inside, she was awestruck by the opulence of the royal residence, but also, *terrified*.

Why would the king summon me?

All too soon, and to her dismay, she understood. Thinking back on that night now, her cheeks burned in shame.

When, a few weeks later, she realized she was pregnant, she sent a panic-stricken message to the king with the news. He promptly called Uriah home from battle, hoping to hide his sin under the guise of a legitimate pregnancy. Uriah, however, possessed a depth of honor that alluded King David. Feeling compelled to resist the comforts of home while his fellow soldiers risked their lives, he laid his mat alongside the palace servants rather than return home to his wife.

When David realized his scheme had failed, he turned to a more drastic—and deadly—solution. He sent word to his commander, Joab, to place Uriah up front in the battle where the fighting was the fiercest, then pull the other fighters back from him, abandoning him to die.

Bathsheba shook her head, trying to clear it of the painful memories, as she pushed the needle and thread through the fabric one last time, closing the tear completely. Then, she stood, slipped the undergarment over her head, and stifled a sob.

A moment later, her few belongings by her side, she waited by the door for one of the king's servants to come take her to the palace. There, to hide the true nature of her pregnancy, she would become David's wife.

Justice, it seemed, would remain forever out of reach . . .

Scripture Reading

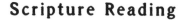

Read the passage below for the account of how Bathsheba lost her husband and became the wife of King David.

II Samuel 11:1–27 NIV

In the spring, at the time when kings go off to war, David sent Joab out with the king's men and the whole Israelite army. They destroyed the Ammonites and besieged Rabbah. But David remained in Jerusalem.

One evening David got up from his bed and walked around on the roof of the palace. From the roof he saw a woman bathing. The woman was very beautiful, and David sent someone to find out about her. The man said, "She is Bathsheba, the daughter of Eliam and the wife of Uriah the Hittite." Then David sent messengers to get her. She came to him, and he slept with her. (Now she was purifying herself from her monthly uncleanness.) Then she went back home. The woman conceived and sent word to David, saying, "I am pregnant."

So David sent this word to Joab: "Send me Uriah the Hittite." . . . When Uriah came to him, David asked him how Joab was, how the soldiers were and how the war was going. Then David said to Uriah, "Go down to your house and wash your feet." So Uriah left the palace, and a gift from the king was sent after him. But Uriah slept at the entrance to the palace with all his master's servants and did not go down to his house . . .

In the morning David wrote a letter to Joab and sent it with Uriah. In it he wrote, "Put Uriah out in front where the fighting is fiercest. Then withdraw from him so he will be struck down and die."

So while Joab had the city under siege, he put Uriah at a place where he knew the strongest defenders were. When the men of the city came out and fought against Joab, some of the men in David's army fell; moreover, Uriah the Hittite died.

Joab sent David a full account of the battle . . .

The messenger set out, and when he arrived he told David everything Joab had sent him to say. The messenger said to David, "The men overpowered us and came out against us in the open, but we drove them back to the entrance of the city gate. Then the archers shot arrows at your servants from the wall, and some of the king's men died. Moreover, your servant Uriah the Hittite is dead."

David told the messenger, "Say this to Joab: 'Don't let this upset you; the sword devours one as well as another. Press the attack against the city and destroy it.' Say this to encourage Joab."

When Uriah's wife heard that her husband was dead, she mourned for him. After the time of mourning was over, David had her brought to his house, and she became his wife and bore him a son. But the thing David had done displeased the Lord.

Let's Review

The first verse of our reading gives us important information about why David saw Bathsheba bathing on the roof. Where was David supposed to be instead of lounging at home?

How does it make you feel when you consider that Bathsheba was powerless to refuse the king's advances?

In a culture where a woman's infidelity was punished with stoning, how do you imagine Bathsheba felt when she realized she was pregnant?

Application

In reading this story, it is easy to get caught up in the sordid details.

A woman bathing on the roof . . .

A king, who should have been off to war, watching her . . .

An unwanted pregnancy . . .

Murder . . .

But the verse in today's reading that matters most is the very last one: "But the thing David had done displeased the Lord."

Bathsheba has, at times, been painted as a lascivious woman for bathing on the roof; however, not only was she not afforded the convenience of indoor plumbing, but it was also not uncommon in her culture to use the roof as an additional, much cooler, room. Furthermore, she had every reason to expect that the king would go off to war with his troops.

As a woman, and a commoner, Bathsheba was powerless in this situation. When the king called, she was obliged to answer. Everything that followed that moment was a tragedy for her.

Not only was she the victim of the king's sexual advances (resulting in an illegitimate pregnancy), but King David also murdered her husband to cover up his sin. Considering that the king was the highest court in the land, Bathsheba had nowhere to turn for justice.

Which brings us to the most important verse in our reading: "But the thing David had done displeased the Lord." God saw it all, and He was ready and willing to hold David accountable for his actions.

Even today, many women live in communities in which they have far less power than men. Sadly, this makes them vulnerable to exploitation and abuse. Whenever possible, we have a responsibility to advocate for and defend these women. There will always be moments, however, when, like Bathsheba, we reach the limit of our abilities to bring about justice for the oppressed. Let us never forget that we can entrust these injustices to God, knowing that He sees, He cares, and He has the power to make a difference.

her heart was shattered

Prompt

Have you or someone you loved suffered an injustice for which it seems there is no human resolution? Write a prayer taking the situation to God.

Dig Deeper

II Samuel 12:1–10
Psalm 64:5–7
Psalm 5:4–6

DAY 14

Tamar, Sister of Absalom

Warning: Survivors of sexual assault may find today's study triggering.

Her hands trembled as she shaped the dough.

Tamar was a young girl, a princess, sent by her father the king to prepare food for her oldest brother, Amnon, who was gravely ill. She obeyed without question, of course, but something wasn't right.

Amnon's eyes never left her as she worked. They looked feverish, crazed . . . but the deep warning bell in Tamar's heart told her his ailment was far more serious than that of a physical nature.

Amnon felt . . . *dangerous.*

When the cakes were cooked, Tamar sighed with relief and placed them before her brother, eager to leave that place and return to the safety of her own home. But he refused to eat.

Instead, he ordered everyone else to leave so that they were alone, then he instructed her to bring the cakes into his chambers. Hesitantly, Tamar followed him into his room as she was told. Her older brother was the firstborn son of the king. How could she refuse?

Tamar watched as he lay down on his bed. Then he told her to bring the food to him where he lay. Her heart pounded in her chest as she timidly stepped closer. Shakily, she held out the cake to him.

Then, in a flash, he grasped her small wrist. Instinctively, she attempted to pull back from him, but it was no use. He was so much stronger than she.

Tamar begged him to let her go. She tried to reason with him, turn him from his lustful obsession. She spoke of shame and dishonor, both hers and his, if he forced himself on her. She even tried to manipulate him into asking their father for her legitimately in marriage, anything to buy herself a moment to escape to safety.

But Amnon foolishly disregarded her wisdom.

He wanted what he wanted. He had the power to take it. And so, he did.

When the assault was over, Amnon called for his servant and had his sister thrown out into the street, bolting the door behind her.

Tamar, battered and bleeding, looked down at her beautiful, ornate robe—a robe fit for a princess of Israel. She grasped the collar, and with a strength fueled by trauma and grief, tore it.

Then she held her head in her hands in mourning . . . and *screamed*.

Scripture Reading

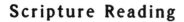

Read the account below of Amnon's assault of his half-sister Tamar.

II Samuel 13:1–19 NRSVA

Some time passed. David's son Absalom had a beautiful sister whose name was Tamar, and David's son Amnon fell in love with her. Amnon was so tormented that he made himself ill because of his sister Tamar, for she was a virgin, and it seemed impossible to Amnon to do anything to her. But Amnon had a friend whose name was Jonadab, the son of David's brother Shimeah, and Jonadab was a very crafty man. He said to him, "O son of the king, why are you so haggard morning after morning? Will you not tell me?" Amnon said to him, "I love Tamar, my brother Absalom's sister." Jonadab said to him, "Lie down on your bed and pretend to be ill, and when your father comes to see you, say to him, 'Let my sister Tamar come and give me something to eat and prepare the food in my sight, so that I may see it and eat it from her hand.'" So Amnon lay down and pretended to be ill, and when the king came to see him, Amnon said to the king, "Please let my sister Tamar come and make a couple of cakes in my sight, so that I may eat from her hand."

Then David sent home to Tamar, saying, "Go to your brother Amnon's house and prepare food for him." So Tamar went to her brother Amnon's house, where he was lying down. She took dough, kneaded it, made cakes in his sight, and baked the cakes. Then she took the pan and set them before him, but he refused to eat. Amnon said, "Send out everyone from me." So everyone went out from him. Then Amnon said to Tamar, "Bring the food into the chamber so that I may eat from your hand." So Tamar took the cakes she had made and brought them into the chamber to Amnon her brother. But when she brought them near him to eat, he took hold of her and said to her, "Come, lie with me, my sister." She answered him, "No, my brother, do not force me, for such a thing is not done in Israel; do not do anything so vile! As for me, where could I carry my shame? And as for you, you would be as one of the scoundrels in Israel. Now therefore, I beg you, speak to the king, for he will not withhold me from you." But he would not listen to her, and being stronger than she, he forced her and lay with her.

Then Amnon was seized with a very great loathing for her; indeed, his loathing was even greater than the lust he had felt for her. Amnon said to her, "Get out!" But she said to him, "No, my brother, for this wrong in sending me away is greater than the other that you did to me." But he would not listen to her. He called the young man who served him and said, "Put this woman out of my presence and bolt the door after her." (Now she was wearing an ornamented robe with sleeves, for this is how the virgin daughters of the king were clothed in earlier times.) So his servant put her out and bolted the door after her. But Tamar put ashes on her head and tore the long robe that she was wearing; she put her hand on her head and went away, crying aloud as she went.

Let's Review

Amnon most certainly knew the story of his father's indulgence and his sexual obsession with Bathsheba. How do you think this influenced his own mindset about whether he was entitled to take what he wanted simply because he had the power to do so?

In today's Scripture reading, David clearly favors his firstborn son, Amnon, over his daughter, Tamar. How does it make you feel to know that David "became very angry, but he would not punish his son Amnon because he loved him, for he was his firstborn" (v. 21)?

Ultimately, Absalom kills Amnon in revenge for the rape of his sister. How might the situation have turned out differently if David had held himself to a higher standard of justice?

Application

When we find Tamar in today's story, a young girl of perhaps only twelve or thirteen years old, her wrist in the steely grip of her powerful oldest brother, she is in crisis.

Tamar uses the resources at her disposal, her wisdom and character, to attempt to dissuade Amnon. She pleads with him to turn away from his sexual obsession. She warns him that her incestuous rape will bear the fruits of shame and destruction for everyone involved.

But these are the limits of Tamar's resources. Amnon is physically stronger than she, and as the oldest son of the king, he holds a place of favor and privilege that are far beyond her own. What is more, Amnon has learned from his own father's example with Bathsheba that, as a powerful man, he is entitled to take what he wants.

Tamar is the voice of godly wisdom, but Amnon is foolish, given wholly over to the indulgences of his own sexual impulses. He feels entitled to have what he wants. When he is finished, he casts her out into the street and bolts the door behind her.

The picture here is stark. Tamar stands outside the barred door of her brother's home, tears her richly ornamented robe, holds her head in her hands in mourning, and wails loudly. She is violated. Bruised, bleeding, and utterly broken.

And this is where we leave Tamar. Sadly, she will find no justice in her father, King David. Instead, she will live as a desolate woman in the home of her brother, Absalom. Because of the stigma rape carries in her culture, it is unlikely she will ever marry, have children, or oversee a home of her own.

As we read Tamar's story, we are faced with the hard truth that there are some injustices we or those we love suffer that fall far beyond any hope of human remedy. Justice in these instances is a work of God alone.

His arm is never "too short to save, nor his ear too dull to hear" (Isaiah 59:1 niv). We can entrust our injustices to Him.

He bends low to *hear* our cries

Prompt

Is there an injustice in your life that seems beyond the hope of any human remedy? Take a moment to pour out your sorrow to God, asking Him to faithfully bring forth justice.

Dig Deeper

Proverb 22:8
Isaiah 58:6
Psalm 94:12–15

DAY 15

Esther

Queen Esther stood in the shadows at the entrance to the inner court of the palace and carefully smoothed barely visible wrinkles from her royal robes. Then, she closed her eyes, willing her racing heart to still.

Had it been only three days since Mordecai sent word to her that the lives of her people hung in the balance and challenged her to approach the king on their behalf? It seemed like a lifetime since she held the copy of the royal edict in her hands announcing the approaching slaughter of every Jewish man, woman, and child living in Persian exile.

Mordecai was convinced that she, Esther, was their best hope. He sent word to her through a servant, instructing her to go before the king and beg for mercy.

But there was one small problem: by law, anyone who approached the king apart from his summoning was subject to immediate execution unless the king extended his golden scepter to them, indicating his favor. Esther was far from confident that she still held her husband's favor. It had been thirty days since he had called for her. With each day that passed, her position felt more precarious.

She sent a message back to Mordecai expressing her fears. His return response was unyielding:

"Do not think that because you are in the king's house you alone of all the Jews will escape," he warned. "For if you remain silent at this time, relief and deliverance for the Jews will arise from another place, but you and your father's family will perish. And who knows but that you have come to your royal position for such a time as this?"

Esther's royal position had come at great cost. When the king grew unhappy with his former queen, he discarded her and began gathering the most beautiful women from his kingdom into his royal harem. Some were Persians. Others, like Esther, were Jewish captives of war living in exile in a foreign land.

Esther was taken from all she knew and everyone she loved to become part of the king's harem. After a year of extensive beauty treatments, she and the other young women were presented to the king for him to choose his next queen. His eye landed on her. After which, she bore the weight of a golden crown on her head, royal robes on her back, and a life that would never again be her own.

She was terrified, but she couldn't escape Mordecai's challenge to courageously do what she could to save her people.

And who knows but that you have come to your royal position for such a time as this?

Esther took one more deep breath and stepped into the sunlit courtyard. Immediately, her eyes met those of the king's where he sat on his throne in the royal hall, directly across from the door to the courtyard.

The guards on each side of the throne tensed as they gripped the handles of their weapons, prepared to relieve her of her head. Time seemed to stand still as Esther stood trembling in the courtyard, her eyes on the king's.

Then, he lifted his golden scepter toward her, indicating his favor. Shakily, Esther walked forward until she was close enough to touch the tip of the scepter with her finger.

"What is it, Queen Esther?" the king asked. "What is your request? Even up to half the kingdom, it will be given you."

Scripture Reading

Read the passage below for the scriptural account of how Esther risked her life to save her people.

Esther 4:7–5:3 NIV

Mordecai told [Hathak] everything that had happened to him, including the exact amount of money Haman had promised to pay into the royal treasury for the destruction of the Jews. He also gave him a copy of the text of the edict for their annihilation, which had been published in Susa, to show to Esther and explain it to her, and he told him to instruct her to go into the king's presence to beg for mercy and plead with him for her people.

Hathak went back and reported to Esther what Mordecai had said. Then she instructed him to say to Mordecai, "All the king's officials and the people of the royal provinces know that for any man or woman who approaches the king in the inner court without being summoned the king has but one law: that they be put to death unless the king extends the gold scepter to them and spares their lives. But thirty days have passed since I was called to go to the king."

When Esther's words were reported to Mordecai, he sent back this answer: "Do not think that because you are in the king's house you alone of all the Jews will escape. For if you remain silent at this time, relief and deliverance for the Jews will arise from another place, but you and your father's family will perish. And who knows but that you have come to your royal position for such a time as this?"

Then Esther sent this reply to Mordecai: "Go, gather together all the Jews who are in Susa, and fast for me. Do not eat or drink for three days, night or day. I and my attendants will fast as you do. When this is done, I will go to the king, even though it is against the law. And if I perish, I perish."

So Mordecai went away and carried out all of Esther's instructions.

On the third day Esther put on her royal robes and stood in the inner court of the palace, in front of the king's hall. The king was sitting on his royal throne in the hall, facing the entrance. When he saw Queen Esther standing in the court, he was pleased with her and held out to her the gold scepter that was in his hand. So Esther approached and touched the tip of the scepter.

Then the king asked, "What is it, Queen Esther? What is your request? Even up to half the kingdom, it will be given you."

Let's Review

Esther, a young Jewish woman, was taken into a foreign king's harem and, eventually, made queen. From the moment she passed through the palace gates, she had little power over her own life. What emotions do you think Esther might have experienced when she was taken into the king's harem?

When Esther's adopted father, Mordecai, instructs her to approach the king on behalf of the Jews, she is understandably afraid. Mordecai, however, calls her to courage and action. How important do you think it is for us to challenge each other to serve God with boldness?

Esther agrees to go before the king to advocate for her people, but first, she asks the Jews to fast and pray for her. What does this tell you about where Esther found the source of her strength and courage?

Application

Have you ever found yourself in a moment in which all hope has been extinguished and you wondered how God could ever bring about redemption and resurrection for you?

Esther's story offers us the hope that no matter how dark the moment in which we find ourselves, God has the power to redeem our struggles—and our sufferings—for His purposes and His glory.

Esther was a queen, but the golden bracelets on her wrists were shackles. Her life, her very body, was not her own. Once she entered the palace gates for the first time as a young Jewish woman, she existed solely for the king's pleasure.

Until, that is, God determined otherwise.

God granted Esther favor with the king and empowered her to advocate for her people. Through her spirit-filled efforts, the Jews were saved.

Esther's story shows us how to navigate the dark and treacherous landscape of trials:

1. Face the situation honestly. Esther was fully aware of the precariousness of her situation.

2. Listen carefully to trusted friends and family when they challenge us to boldly play our part in advancing the kingdom of God.

3. Recognize that we are wholly dependent on the Spirit's power. Esther fasted and prayed for three days before she approached the king and asked the women in her court, along with all the Jews in Persia, to fast with her.

When we live our lives sincerely, boldly following the Lord's leading, we can be confident that He will bring about our good and His glory from even the most daunting circumstances.

for such a time as this

Prompt

Is there a "Mordecai" in your life who challenges you to live boldly for God? Take time to thank God for this person. If you don't have a "Mordecai," ask God to bring that person into your life.

Dig Deeper

Proverbs 28:1
Ephesians 6:10–19
Matthew 10:16–42

DAY 16

Mary's Unplanned Pregnancy

Thirteen years—the short span of one young girl's lifetime, and yet long enough to paint a vision of her future so vividly that she could see all the tiny details each time she closed her eyes.

Her wedding garments.

The sound of the groom's joyful procession as it neared her childhood home.

Joseph's eyes when he saw her, his bride, for the first time.

The shouts and songs of her entire village as they accompanied the bridal party to Joseph's family home.

A feast that stretched on for days.

Now, it all lay in ashes at her feet, her dreams set alight by the angel Gabriel's announcement.

He had called her "highly favored," and so, despite her fear, it must be true. Gabriel said she would have a son, even though she was a virgin, and that this son, Jesus, would inherit the throne of King David, a kingdom without end.

But who would believe her? Wouldn't Joseph assume her infidelity and break their engagement? Would she not have her offense announced in the street, bringing shame on her and her family?

Would the neighbors whom she had known since she was a baby come to her door with stones in their hands to take her and her unborn son's lives?

"Don't be afraid," Gabriel had said.

She wanted to be brave—wanted to say "yes" to God's dream for her—but there were moments when it felt like not only her dreams, but her world, had been utterly destroyed and that she was the only one in on the secret so far.

Gabriel must have seen the terror in her eyes, the trembling of her hands, because he offered her a sweet consolation. Her cousin, Elizabeth, who was far past the age to conceive a child, was in her sixth month of pregnancy.

"For no word from God will ever fail," Gabriel had said.

And so, young Mary lifted her eyes from the ashes of her dreams, the unrecognizable remnant of the person she always imagined she would be, and opened her hands to receive God's dream for her instead.

Perhaps she would never become Joseph's wife. Maybe her future was one of shame instead of honor—the steep price of divine favor. But she was confident in who God was and that she was His.

Shaking voice.

Trembling hands.

And a courageous proclamation of faith . . .

"I am the Lord's servant," she said to Gabriel. "May your word to me be fulfilled."

99

Scripture Reading

Read Luke's account of the angel Gabriel's visit to Mary.

Luke 1:26–38 NIV

In the sixth month of Elizabeth's pregnancy, God sent the angel Gabriel to Nazareth, a town in Galilee, to a virgin pledged to be married to a man named Joseph, a descendant of David. The virgin's name was Mary. The angel went to her and said, "Greetings, you who are highly favored! The Lord is with you."

Mary was greatly troubled at his words and wondered what kind of greeting this might be. But the angel said to her, "Do not be afraid, Mary; you have found favor with God. You will conceive and give birth to a son, and you are to call Him Jesus. He will be great and will be called the Son of the Most High. The Lord God will give Him the throne of His father David, and He will reign over Jacob's descendants forever; His kingdom will never end."

"How will this be," Mary asked the angel, "since I am a virgin?"

The angel answered, "The Holy Spirit will come on you, and the power of the Most High will overshadow you. So the holy one to be born will be called the Son of God. Even Elizabeth your relative is going to have a child in her old age, and she who was said to be unable to conceive is in her sixth month. For no word from God will ever fail."

"I am the Lord's servant," Mary answered. "May your word to me be fulfilled." Then the angel left her.

Let's Review

Mary was in the middle of an exciting time of her life—her betrothal—when God interrupted her life with a new purpose all His own. Have you ever experienced a "divine interruption"? If so, how did you handle it? If not, what struggles do you imagine Mary had during this time?

When Gabriel brought Mary this message that would turn her life upside down, he also encouraged her with the news of her cousin Elizabeth's unlikely pregnancy. When you read this portion of the passage, how does the angel's promise that "no word from God will ever fail" bring you hope today?

God's mission for Mary was far from easy. She knew this all too well, and yet, in an act of tremendous faith, she responds, "I am the Lord's servant. May your word to me be fulfilled." How does Mary's courage, faith, and strength inspire your own?

Application

Some dreams are more precious than others because they are the foundation of the lives we have envisioned for ourselves. These dreams are more than what we will do or where we will be. They are a snapshot of who we think we are . . . our vision of our future selves.

For many of us, these core identity dreams begin forming early in childhood. So often, we love to ask children what they want to be when they grow up. And so, when we are barely out of diapers, we begin to fashion a treasured image of our future selves.

Most of the time, these dreams ebb and flow, transitioning from one passion to another as we grow and change; but occasionally, a childhood dream has staying power—such unwavering resiliency that a person reaches the threshold of adulthood with it still intact. When a dream like that crumbles, its loss is painful indeed.

This must have been what it was like for Mary. When Gabriel appeared to her, Mary likely lost the only vision of her future self she had ever had, and the one God offered her in return must have seemed so dangerous that her very survival felt at risk.

Sometimes, God's best for us comes at the cost of the dream we hold most dear. The choice before us in that moment is whether we will fight God's dream for us, clinging painfully to the long-treasured vision of our future until we are exhausted, or will we grieve its loss and, like Mary, open our hands to receive God's plan for our lives instead?

The key, perhaps, is what we believe about the nature of God.

Do we believe He is loving, faithful, generous, and kind? Do we believe He is only good? When we do, we find the courage to echo Mary's faithful proclamation, made when her own dreams lay in tatters at her feet:

"I am the Lord's servant. May your word to me be fulfilled."

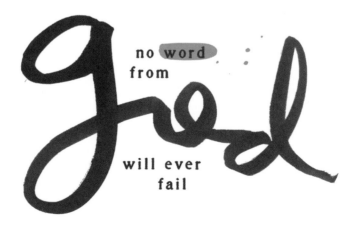

no word from god will ever fail

Prompt

Write a prayer asking God to give you a courageous faith like Mary's.

Dig Deeper

Luke 1:46–55
Isaiah 7:14
Isaiah 9:1–7

DAY 17

Elizabeth, Believer of God's Promises

First, there was a sense of fullness in her lower abdomen. Then, several weeks later, a faint fluttering as gentle as the brush of a butterfly's wing.

After that, the sense of movement grew steadily stronger. A rolling sensation here. A firm little kick there.

Throughout the day, Elizabeth's hand drifted to the place, protectively cradling her swelling belly. At night, she took Zechariah's hand and placed it over the place where his unborn son grew, slept, and sucked his thumb in the dark, secret place of her womb, and watched with joy as the old man's eyes lit up with each roll and kick.

For five months, she stayed in seclusion, holding the secret of God's miraculous gift close, knowing the uproar that would occur when the news spread like wildfire among her neighbors and friends:

Elizabeth, old enough to be a grandmother, is expecting a child!

Then, one day in her sixth month, her young cousin, Mary, arrived unexpectedly for a visit. When she walked in the gate and called out to Elizabeth in greeting, the baby in her womb leaped!

Filled with the power of the Holy Spirit, Elizabeth, prophesied: "Blessed are you among women, and blessed is the child you will bear! But why am I so favored, that the mother of my Lord should come to me? As soon as the sound of your greeting reached my ears, the baby in my womb leaped for joy. Blessed is she who has believed that the Lord would fulfill His promises to her!"

Blessed is she who has believed that the Lord would fulfill His promises to her.

Elizabeth knew all too well the challenge of holding onto God's promises when everything she saw, and heard, dared her to abandon faith. For years, she had clung to God's promise of a child while she and Zechariah grew old, and everyone around her speculated that her barrenness was the result of some secret sin.

But still she held fast. She kept her eyes on the Creator of all.

And now, a flutter and a kick. Gray hair at her temples and a swelling abdomen beneath her robe.

A leaping baby in her womb, filled with the Holy Spirit even before he was born.

Elizabeth believed, and she was blessed indeed.

Scripture Reading

Below read Luke's account of Mary's visit to Elizabeth.

Luke 1:24–25, 39–45 NIV

After this his wife Elizabeth became pregnant and for five months remained in seclusion. "The Lord has done this for me," she said. "In these days He has shown His favor and taken away my disgrace among the people."

***

At that time Mary got ready and hurried to a town in the hill country of Judea, where she entered Zechariah's home and greeted Elizabeth. When Elizabeth heard Mary's greeting, the baby leaped in her womb, and Elizabeth was filled with the Holy Spirit. In a loud voice she exclaimed: "Blessed are you among women, and blessed is the child you will bear! But why am I so favored, that the mother of my Lord should come to me? As soon as the sound of your greeting reached my ears, the baby in my womb leaped for joy. Blessed is she who has believed that the Lord would fulfill His promises to her!"

Let's Review

In Elizabeth's culture, barrenness was considered punishment from God. Luke 1:6 (NIV) is careful to tell us that this was not the case for Zechariah and Elizabeth, that they were "righteous in the sight of God, observing all the Lord's commands and decrees blamelessly." How do you imagine her neighbors' assumptive judgment added to Elizabeth's suffering?

As we consider Elizabeth's plight, and her community's likely response, how do you think we can better love those in our community who are going through a season of suffering?

When Elizabeth greeted Mary, she said, "Blessed is she who has believed that the Lord would fulfill His promises to her!" (Luke 1:45 NIV). How do you think Elizabeth's own courageous belief helped encourage Mary?

Application

The early days of belief are easy, but the long years of belief, waiting throughout the seasons for the fulfillment of God's promises, are hard.

How do we hold on to hope when the realization of God's sweetest assurances to us linger beyond all that seems reasonable?

Scripture doesn't tell us Elizabeth's secret of faith. We do know that her husband, Zechariah, struggled to believe even when an angel appeared to him before the altar of incense in the temple. God granted him nine months of silent contemplation to consider the mystery.

Perhaps the secret of believing, when the years slip by as we wait for God's promise, is found in the small practices woven into a life of faith. We pray. Spend time contemplating the Scriptures. We encourage each other, believing *for* each other when our brothers and sisters grow weary in waiting.

Then, when the moment of fulfillment finally comes, we rejoice with each other.

Luke 1:65–66 (NIV) gives us sweet insight into the power of a promise fulfilled within a community of faith.

> *All the neighbors were filled with awe [after Elizabeth gave birth to John], and throughout the hill country of Judea people were talking about all these things. Everyone who heard this wondered about it, asking, "What then is this child going to be?" For the Lord's hand was with him.*

The miracle of John's birth in Elizabeth's old age challenged her entire community to believe bigger of God. They probably thought, *if God could do this, who knows what He might be up to next?*

Indeed, who knows? For He is limitless and unpredictable in His wonder. He is extravagant, generous in His gifts. He is the God of impossible things.

Blessed is she who believes.

He is the God of impossible things

Prompt

Is God calling you to trust that He will fulfill His promises to you? Take time to journal about any challenges you are facing in this area.

Dig Deeper

Mark 9:14–24
Hebrews 11:1–3
Luke 1:5–25

Mary Gives Birth

Note: Many of us grew up hearing about the night Jesus was born and how there was "no room in the inn." The Greek word for "inn," a place in which a traveler could rent a place to stay the night, is "pandocheion." The word traditionally translated "inn" in the nativity story, however, is "kataluma" which means, "guest room." Mary and Joseph returned to Bethlehem for the census because it was Joseph's hometown, so it would make sense that he had family there! Since everyone was required to return to their hometowns for the census, Joseph's family would have been managing a full house and there would have been no room in the "kataluma," or "guest room," for Mary to give birth privately. The narrative below puts the scene of Jesus's birth at Joseph's relatives house.

She is fourteen years old and far from home when the first labor pains strike. The house where she and her husband, Joseph, are staying is full to overflowing. They, along with many members of Joseph's extended family, have come to Bethlehem from all over Israel for the census. And while the census left little to celebrate, the reuniting of family was always sweet.

But she is new to this family, young and heavily pregnant. When the first wave of pain is followed a few minutes later by another, and it is clear that the moment has come for her to give birth, she must have longed for her own mother.

It didn't take long for the older women who were present to read the signs—her forehead glistening with sweat, her face creased in pain, her breathing rapid.

One woman moves to her side while another gives orders to the men to move the animals out of the basement stables and put down clean straw. Still another whispers words of comfort and peace to Joseph before sending him on his way.

This is woman's work—the holy work of bringing life into the world.

Another contraction, and Mary cries out. Women surround her, and strong arms lead her downstairs to the stables. For hours, Mary shuffles along the perimeter of the space as calm voices whisper encouragement.

When the moment arrives for Jesus to be born, they help her to the birthing stool. One wipes her forehead, another kneels beside her, eyes on hers, helping her manage her breathing. The midwife crouches in front of her, experienced hands ready to receive new life.

Together, they lend Mary their courage and strength for the final moments of childbirth.

Yes, yes, you can do this . . .

Just one more push. He's almost here.

You are stronger than you know. It is almost over . . .

Hands grip hers as she cries out one last time, and then, a miracle slips quietly from eternity and into the world He helped speak into existence. After a brief moment of silence, the newborn fills His lungs with air for the first time and cries.

There are shouts of elation from the stables, matched with shouts of celebration from the room above. Mary sheds joyful tears as she pulls her son to her breast. He latches on and quiets. She runs her fingers through his dark curls, and as she does, she remembers the angel Gabriel's words:

"Do not be afraid, Mary. You have found favor with God . . ."

And looking into Jesus's eyes as He nurses for the first time, Mary knows in the depths of her being that it is true.

Scripture Reading

Take a moment to read Luke's account of Jesus's birth.

Luke 2:1–7 NIV

In those days Caesar Augustus issued a decree that a census should be taken of the entire Roman world. (This was the first census that took place while Quirinius was governor of Syria.) And everyone went to their own town to register.

So Joseph also went up from the town of Nazareth in Galilee to Judea, to Bethlehem the town of David, because he belonged to the house and line of David. He went there to register with Mary, who was pledged to be married to him and was expecting a child. While they were there, the time came for the baby to be born, and she gave birth to her firstborn, a Son. She wrapped Him in cloths and placed Him in a manger, because there was no guest room available for them.

Let's Review

The belief that the Jews were a nation belonging to God alone was woven into Israel's national identity. Therefore, this census by an occupying nation, for the purpose of the taxation of their ancestral lands, felt to many Jews like a fresh descent into slavery. (See Antiquities, Book XVIII, Josephus.) How does this bit of information add weight to the timing of Jesus's birth? (See Luke 4:18 for a hint.)

Our reading tells us that Joseph "belonged to the house and line of David" (Luke 2:4 NIV). David was Israel's greatest monarch. Have you ever thought about the fact that Joseph was from the royal line? What significance does this hold for Jesus as his adopted son?

Most of us grew up hearing "there was no room in the inn." The word traditionally translated as in "inn" is actually the word "kataluma" which is translated to mean, "guest room." How does this change your image of the circumstances surrounding Jesus's birth?

Application

The details included in Scripture surrounding the birth of Jesus are heavy with significance. When Augustus issued the decree for the Jews to return to their hometowns to be counted, the Jews would have seen it as an aggressive act of dominance by an occupying force.

What an incredible moment for the Messiah to be born. The expectation of the Jews was that the long-foretold Messiah would come to set His people free from oppression. In their minds, this meant casting the Romans out of Judea so that Israel might once again enjoy self-rule.

God, however, had a bigger redemption in mind in the Messiah. The purpose of Jesus's coming was greater than that of delivering the Jews from physical oppression—He came to break the curse of sin, redeeming all of creation from the fall.

Another sweet detail to take note of: homes in the first century were two story structures. Upon entrance of the front door, one might go either up a short flight of stairs to the main room of the home or down to the stables beneath that area. (Yes, both animals and people entered the home through the same door!)

Once upstairs, the structure was one large living area open to the stables below. At the edge of the floor between the main room and the stable area, mangers were carved into the floor so that hungry livestock might stick their heads up over the edge for a snack during the night.

These mangers made convenient cradles for newborn peasant babies. When Scripture reveals the detail that Jesus slept in one of these "manger cradles," the implication is that the King of the Universe came as a peasant baby. The detail that Mary wrapped Him in cloths is another indication of this, as this was how peasant families, including shepherds, clothed their newborns.

With everyone returning to their hometowns for the census, it stands to reason that the guest room was full of family and therefore, unavailable to the laboring mother for childbirth. Moving Mary to the stable below to give birth afforded her much needed privacy.

What a beautiful picture of Jesus's entry into the world! Surely, Mary was surrounded by loving, older women who helped her give birth as women have done for each other throughout the centuries.

How beautiful it is to realize how the story of Jesus's birth proclaims over and again that He humbled Himself in every way to restore us to God the Father. He left His home in glory, took on fragile infant flesh, cast Himself in full dependence on a peasant girl for survival, and chose a manger as His cradle.

God not only entrusted a fourteen-year-old peasant girl from Nazareth to bring the Messiah into the world but to protect and nurture Him until He reached adulthood. Could there be any greater testimony concerning God's deep esteem of women?

Prompt

Take a moment to write a prayer of thanks for the courage of young Mary and her faithful love and care for the Messiah.

Dig Deeper

Psalm 127:3
Psalm 113:9
Matthew 1:20–22

DAY 19

The Canaanite Woman

"Have mercy on me, Lord, Son of David; my daughter is tormented by a demon," the desperate mother cried.

When the group of men before her turned toward her, all but One looked at her with open disgust. But she wasn't speaking to them—she was pleading with Him, *the One*, for mercy.

Jesus's eyes, compassionate and kind, searched hers for a moment before turning to face His disciples. For a long moment He searched their faces, marked with disdain, then their hearts, bound by bigotry.

There was so much promise in the men before Him, the future leaders of the church, but they were flawed too—sinful men chosen to lead other sinners into the kingdom of God. Their vision for that kingdom was far too small to include a foreign woman like the one standing before them.

"Send her away," His disciples demanded, "for she keeps coming after us."

Jesus looked back at the mother, her eyes filled with tears, as she begged for her daughter's freedom and healing. Then He looked deeper into her heart too.

Such love, courage, and faith . . .

Perhaps she could help Him expose His disciples' flawed beliefs—the thin, loveless, vein of prejudice that ran through their minds and hearts.

"I was sent only to the lost sheep of the house of Israel," He said softly.

Behind Him, a murmur of approval rippled through the disciples as they each stood a bit taller, chests out and chins up.

The mother simply took a few steps forward, and knelt in the dirt before Jesus, her eyes never leaving His.

"Lord, help me," she said.

A weeping mother was on her knees begging for her little girl's life, and *somehow*, His disciples remained unmoved by her suffering.

Jesus pushed the lesson still further, speaking aloud the dark beliefs hidden in their hearts.

"It is not fair to take the children's food and throw it to the dogs," he replied.

The woman was not dissuaded.

"Yes, Lord, yet even the dogs eat the crumbs that fall from their master's table."

Jesus laughed softly, delighted by her response.

"Woman, great is your faith!" He said. "Let it be done for you as you wish."

A daughter freed. Her mother, a foreigner, honored for her faith.

And the disciples taught a valuable lesson about just how far their own hearts were from the kingdom of God.

Scripture Reading

Read the passage below for the account of the Canaanite woman's interaction with Jesus.

Matthew 15:21–28 NRSVA

Jesus left that place and went away to the district of Tyre and Sidon. Just then a Canaanite woman from that region came out and started shouting, "Have mercy on me, Lord, Son of David; my daughter is tormented by a demon." But He did not answer her at all. And His disciples came and urged Him, saying, "Send her away, for she keeps shouting after us." He answered, "I was sent only to the lost sheep of the house of Israel." But she came and knelt before Him, saying, "Lord, help me." He answered, "It is not fair to take the children's food and throw it to the dogs." She said, "Yes, Lord, yet even the dogs eat the crumbs that fall from their masters' table." Then Jesus answered her, "Woman, great is your faith! Let it be done for you as you wish." And her daughter was healed instantly.

Let's Review

The disciples were so blind to their own prejudices against women and "foreigners" that they were oblivious to this mother's suffering. It is easy to pass judgment on them, but we are all vulnerable to "blind spots" when it comes to sin. What steps can you take to search out these areas in your life, bring them to God, and keep them in check?

Jesus's seemingly callous rejection of this mother's cry for help reflected His disciples' sinful attitudes toward her. He was, in essence, shining a spotlight on their hard hearts, entrusting her to help Him teach them a lesson. Have you ever known someone whom God redeemed from their suffering, and then He used the situation to draw others closer to Him? Write briefly about that person's life and what you learned from him or her.

You have to appreciate Jesus's sense of irony. His disciples rejected this woman, deeming her unworthy of their time. So Jesus not only granted her request but also made her their teacher! When you think of how Jesus honored her in this way, how does that make you feel?

Application

The woman in today's story was the least likely person whom the disciples would have ever expected to have as a teacher. Not only did their culture value a man's voice over a woman's, but it was also heavily invested in a belief system of racial superiority. The Jews of Jesus's day felt like they had the only tickets to the kingdom of God. As far as they were concerned, no one else mattered very much.

Jesus had a way of finding faith in the strangest of places: a sinful tax collector named Zacchaeus who balanced in the branches of a tree just for the chance to see Him; a Roman Centurion who came to Him on behalf of his servant who was ill and suffering terribly.

And a woman—a foreigner—who possessed such remarkable spiritual insight that she combined the cry of a beggar with *His Messianic title* when she called out to Him for help.

"Have mercy on me, Lord, *Son of David. . . .*"

As any mother who has watched her child suffer could attest, there is nothing more difficult than waiting for a child's healing. It couldn't have been easy for this mother to stand her ground in the face of Jesus's apparent rejection, even if it was only for a moment. Yet that is what she did, and in doing so, she taught the leaders of the early church, men who would become saints and martyrs.

Never underestimate the impact of a stubborn faith in moments of profound darkness. It may be just the moment your light is shining the most brightly of all.

such love, *courage* & faith

Prompt

Are you, like the woman in today's story, kneeling before Jesus in stubborn faith today? Ask Him to strengthen and comfort you while you await His compassion that never fails.

Dig Deeper

Romans 10:11–13
Galatians 3:27–29
Titus 2:11–12

DAY 20

The Woman Who Gave Her All

All around her was . . . majesty.

The temple complex was breathtaking—the mighty walls surrounding the temple courts, constructed of smooth-hewn stones of inconceivable immensity. The beautiful tiles underneath her feet. The massive Gates of Nicanor which led to the temple itself, radiant in the Middle Eastern sun.

The sounds of sheep bleating and doves cooing, and the harsh cries of merchants haggling over their prices, competed with those of countless voices raised in prayer.

A steady stream of worshippers clothed in fine robes of scarlet and purple held heavy bags of silver and gold in their hands as they made their way to the Court of Women where thirteen collection boxes, the *shofarot*, awaited their offerings. Each collection box was topped with a "shofar-shaped" funnel through which worshippers deposited their offerings. (A *shofar* is a trumpet made from a ram's horn.)

When the heavy bags of silver and gold dropped through the funnel and landed in the box below, it made a loud noise, which is why the act of giving a donation was known as "playing the trumpet."

But this woman, a widow, had no soft, beautiful robe. Instead, she wore the coarse goat's hair garment of mourning. There was no impressive offering in her hand, only two thin copper coins.

It wasn't much, but to her it was everything. It was all she had.

A few more steps and at last, she stood before the *shofarot*. She lifted her hand to the opening of the *shofar* and tilted it so that the small coins fell from her palm and into the depths of the collection box. All around her the other "trumpets" rang noisily as they received their treasures, but her offering was so small that it didn't make a sound. None of the other worshippers even noticed her gift.

But Jesus did.

He turned to His disciples, offering them a lesson in faith and generosity only a poor widow was worthy to teach them.

"Truly I tell you," He said to His disciples, "this poor widow has put in more than all those who are contributing to the treasury. For all of them have contributed out of their abundance, but she out of her poverty has put in everything she had, all she had to live on."

Scripture Reading

Read the passage below to learn more about the widow who gave all she had.

Mark 12:41–44 NRSVA

He sat down opposite the treasury and watched the crowd putting money into the treasury. Many rich people put in large sums. A poor widow came and put in two small copper coins, which are worth a penny. Then He called His disciples and said to them, "Truly I tell you, this poor widow has put in more than all those who are contributing to the treasury. For all of them have contributed out of their abundance, but she out of her poverty has put in everything she had, all she had to live on."

Let's Review

It is easy to imagine that the widow in today's reading must have felt out of place in the opulent temple setting. What do you think motivated her to push any feelings of insecurity aside to offer her gift anyway?

We live in a world that is addicted to image—each post on social media a carefully crafted demonstration of superiority. Consider the competition of "playing the trumpet" in today's reading and Jesus's teaching to His disciples concerning the widow's gift. What principles can you draw from this for navigating the image-conscious culture in which we live?

The widow's gift was meager in comparison to others given that day, yet she didn't hesitate to offer it. What gift do you have to offer Jesus today? (Gifts are not limited to monetary offerings. We can offer Jesus the gift of service too.)

Application

Jesus once said that true worshippers of God worship in "spirit and in truth" (John 4:23–24). Isn't that beautiful?

But . . . it is also risky because whenever we determine to worship God in "spirit and truth," it will take us far outside of our culture's norms. This type of worship casts image to the side, fixing its eyes on God alone.

During Jesus's day, "playing the trumpet" at the temple was much like posting on social media today. While the men and women in the first century didn't have the best ring lighting or latest photo editing software, they did know how to make an impression.

Dressed in their most elegant robes, they dropped their offerings in the *shofarot*, and the sound of their gift hitting the bottom of the box rang throughout the temple courts; everyone present turned their way to see who had made such a large donation.

The affirmation was intoxicating. All-consuming. Addicting.

Enslaving.

Once, Jesus warned His followers to give so discreetly that their left hand would not know what their right hand was doing (Matthew 6:2–4). He knew that seeking the approval of others is a hunger that is forever ravenous, impossible to satisfy.

What about you? Have you fallen into the trap of seeking the approval of others? It is a miserable way to live. Instead, fix your eyes on Jesus and decide that you will seek to please Him alone. In doing so, you will find more joy and peace than you ever thought possible.

spirit & in truth

Prompt

Write a prayer asking God to free you from seeking affirmation from others. Ask Him to fill you with His love and acceptance and guard your heart with His peace.

Dig Deeper

Psalm 132:15
Proverbs 11:25
Matthew 6:2–4

DAY 21

The Widow of Nain

Each step behind the funeral bier, as it made its sorrowful journey to the graveyard on the outskirts of town, was a wound to her soul.

The haunting sound of the mourners' wailing rose ever higher, drowning out the sound of her own sandals on the rock and sand beneath her, until their cries were the only sound in the world.

Rising and falling. Rising and falling. Waves of grief carrying her forward to her only son's grave.

Before her, the image of his body wrapped in grave cloths as it rested on the bier, held aloft by the strong hands of his cousins and uncles, blurred through her tears.

Just that morning, she had held him, strong and tall in her arms. Now, her boy was lost to her forever.

This journey was painfully familiar. She had last walked it for her husband, on the day she became a widow. But there was no name for what she was now, for words fell short to capture the depth of loss for a widow who had also lost her only child.

Just then, a voice filled with compassion spoke to her.

"Don't cry," Jesus said.

Don't cry? How could she ever stop crying ever again?

But before she could voice her protest, Jesus moved away from her to place one hand on the bier, bringing the procession to a standstill. Then He spoke to her dead son.

"Young man, I say to you, get up!"

Immediately, *unbelievably*, her boy sat straight up on the bier and began shaking loose his grave cloths. The crowd erupted in wondrous, joyful praise.

Jesus just smiled and led the young man to his mother.

She cried out in joy as she pulled her boy into her arms.

Warm.

Strong.

The aroma of the burial herbs still clinging to his hair and skin.

But wondrously, fully alive.

Scripture Reading

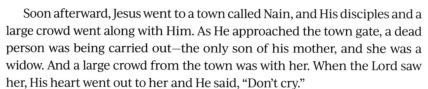

Read the passage below for the account of the widow of Nain's encounter with Jesus.

Luke 7:11–17 NIV

Soon afterward, Jesus went to a town called Nain, and His disciples and a large crowd went along with Him. As He approached the town gate, a dead person was being carried out—the only son of his mother, and she was a widow. And a large crowd from the town was with her. When the Lord saw her, His heart went out to her and He said, "Don't cry."

Then He went up and touched the bier they were carrying him on, and the bearers stood still. He said, "Young man, I say to you, get up!" The dead man sat up and began to talk, and Jesus gave him back to his mother.

They were all filled with awe and praised God. "A great prophet has appeared among us," they said. "God has come to help His people." This news about Jesus spread throughout Judea and the surrounding country.

Let's Review

⦿ ⦿ ⦿ ⦿ ⦿ ⦿ ⦿ ⦿ ⦿ ⦿ ⦿ ⦿ ⦿ ⦿ ⦿

When the widow in our story encounters Jesus, she has suffered unfathomable loss. Jesus, clearly brokenhearted by her sorrow, says to her "Don't cry." What might your reaction have been if someone said this to you on the way to your only son's funeral?

In this widow's culture, women were highly dependent on male relatives for protection and support. As long as this widow's son was living, she had a place in her deceased husband's family. Imagine her circumstances were your own. What fears might you have had for your future?

This miracle happened on the other side of the mountain from another miraculous resurrection in Scripture: when the prophet Elijah raised the widow of Zarephath's son from the dead. The crowd, familiar with the story, would not have missed the significance of Jesus performing a similar miracle in the region (I Kings 17:7–24).

How does the last paragrah of our Scripture reading say they responded?

Application

It is tempting to imagine how well we might weather crushing loss. Most of us would hope that although we would certainly grieve and struggle, that we might do so nobly. We dare hope that in the darkest moments of our lives, that we will find ourselves capable, at least, of clinging to our faith in a way that points others to our source of strength.

But what happens when our losses overwhelm us?

It has been said that God won't give us more than we can handle, but one would be hard pressed to find this sentiment in Scripture. As a matter of fact, there are many stories in the Bible in which men and women find themselves up against circumstances that are far beyond their ability to endure.

Today's story of the widow of Nain is one of these. Widows were among the most vulnerable people in first-century Israel, so much so that the early church considered their care a top priority (I Timothy 5:3).

This widow, however, had the comfort of a son. Until he reached adulthood, she would have a place in her deceased husband's family. Once he was grown, he would provide a home and provision for her.

His death, following his father's death, was a multilayered loss.

There are many reasons this story was included for us in Scripture, but none sweeter than the lesson we learn about how Jesus interacts with this woman in the moment when her loss had swept her away. He doesn't rebuke her for her lack of faith or challenge her to be strong. He is simply moved by her suffering and responds to it with compassion.

May we remember His tender love for her in the moments when we fall under the weight of loss, and offer ourselves, and each other, the same gentle grace.

she cried out in joy

Prompt

Is there a loss in your life that seems too great to bear? Take a moment to write a prayer asking Jesus for His tender compassion. If not, write on behalf of someone else who is grieving.

Dig Deeper

I Corinthians 15:54–55
Romans 8:11
Psalm 18

DAY 22

The Forgiven Woman Who Loved Much

The room was silent except for the sound of her weeping.

She stood before the low triclinium table*, her arms wrapped around her waist, and her shoulders shaking with each sob. The older rabbis, reclining at the table to eat, glared at her darkly, but her eyes were focused only on the young rabbi named Jesus. Slowly, she knelt at His feet.

She and the other "outcasts" had been sitting along the wall when Jesus arrived. Their part in the feast was simple: Be silent. Be still. Be invisible until Simon was ready to feed them as a public demonstration of his generosity.

It was humiliating, of course, but she was accustomed to public shame. It followed her through the city streets and stalked her in the marketplace. Shame and condemnation clung to the heels of a sinful woman like her as closely as her own shadow.

She saw it in every eye that met her own and heard it in a thousand whispered insults.

Rabbi Jesus, however, was different. In His teachings she had found an offering of grace and a path back to God. Her gratitude for that forgiveness was what had brought her to Simon's home, an expensive alabaster jar of perfume hidden in the folds of her robe. She had hoped to move forward and anoint His feet once the servant finished washing them.

But things had not gone according to plan. As she and the other outcasts watched in shock, Simon had refused Jesus a kiss of greeting and then denied Him the customary washing of His feet.

The snub was deliberate. A shocking breach of decorum. Unimaginably offensive.

And the message was clear: Simon and the other rabbis present were unhappy with Jesus's teaching, and they were putting Him in His place.

So, once everyone had reclined at the table, *she* moved to offer Him the kindness and consideration they had refused Him. She knelt at his feet and gave Him all she had. She had no water with which to wash dust and grime away from His feet, so she allowed her tears to fall on them instead. She had no towel with which to dry His feet, so she tugged her head covering loose and dried them with her hair.

Then she opened the alabaster jar and poured the entire contents of costly perfume on His feet, anointing them.

Jesus looked to where His host, Simon, sat in silent judgment.

"Simon, I have something to tell you," Jesus said.

"Tell me, teacher," he said.

Jesus told Simon a parable about two men who each owed money to a creditor, one more than the other. The creditor generously forgave both debts.

"Which man," Jesus asked Simon, "would love the creditor more?"

Simon said that the man who had been forgiven the most probably loved the most as well. Jesus affirmed that this was true.

Jesus explained to Simon that the woman was offering Him her gift as an act of love and gratitude because she understood how much she had been forgiven.

Then Jesus turned His attention back to the woman at His feet.

"Your sins are forgiven," He said gently. "Your faith has saved you; go in peace."

*A triclinium table was a low, u-shaped structure around which diners reclined to eat.

Scripture Reading

Read the Scripture passage below for the account of one forgiven woman's great love for Jesus.

Luke 7:36–50 NIV

When one of the Pharisees invited Jesus to have dinner with him, He went to the Pharisee's house and reclined at the table. A woman in that town who lived a sinful life learned that Jesus was eating at the Pharisee's house, so she came there with an alabaster jar of perfume. As she stood behind Him at His feet weeping, she began to wet His feet with her tears. Then she wiped them with her hair, kissed them and poured perfume on them.

When the Pharisee who had invited Him saw this, he said to himself, "If this man were a prophet, He would know who is touching Him and what kind of woman she is—that she is a sinner."

Jesus answered him, "Simon, I have something to tell you."

"Tell me, teacher," he said.

"Two people owed money to a certain moneylender. One owed him five hundred denarii, and the other fifty. Neither of them had the money to pay him back, so he forgave the debts of both. Now which of them will love him more?"

Simon replied, "I suppose the one who had the bigger debt forgiven."

"You have judged correctly," Jesus said.

Then He turned toward the woman and said to Simon, "Do you see this woman? I came into your house. You did not give Me any water for My feet, but she wet My feet with her tears and wiped them with her hair. You did not give Me a kiss, but this woman, from the time I entered, has not stopped kissing My feet. You did not put oil on My head, but she has poured perfume on My feet. Therefore, I tell you, her many sins have been forgiven—as her great love has shown. But whoever has been forgiven little loves little."

Then Jesus said to her, "Your sins are forgiven."

The other guests began to say among themselves, "Who is this who even forgives sins?"

Jesus said to the woman, "Your faith has saved you; go in peace."

Let's Review

We, as humans, often get distracted by outward appearances. It is easy to get confused about who is "holy" and who is not. What steps can you take to keep your impulse to judge others in check?

The woman's love for Jesus is so important in this story that it is almost a silent character—always present, influencing the sequence of events, teaching the lesson. In their pursuit of holiness, however, the rabbis in our story had somehow lost their love for God.
Why do you think that is, and what implications does this realization have for your own relationship with God?

When the woman in our story witnessed Simon's insulting treatment of Jesus, she used the only resources she had to correct the injustice. She washed His feet with her tears, dried them with her hair, and kissed them. What does her example teach us about our own power—and responsibility—to correct the injustices we witness in our communities?

Application

Proverbs 6:16–19 lists six things God *hates*. Number one?

"Eyes that are arrogant" (Proverbs 6:16 THE MESSAGE).

In today's story, the eyes of the religious leaders are in stark contrast with those of the sinful woman and of Jesus. In their eyes, we find arrogance, judgment, even cruelty.

The "sinful" woman's eyes, however, are the picture of humility. Filled with tears of gratitude, her focus is not on the powerful men reclining around the table, or even herself, but on the feet of the Messiah.

Jesus looks past it all to their hearts. In the woman, He finds gratitude and faith. In Simon, Jesus discovers a spiritual blindness born out of his own self-righteousness. Simon is unable to see the truth; he is no better than the outcasts and beggars lining his wall. They are all sinners in need of grace.

The only proper response to God's great redemption of us is one of humble gratitude. May we seek the Lover of Our Souls today to help us see ourselves as He sees us. Sinful, weak . . .

. . . and extravagantly loved.

your faith has Saved you

Prompt

Ask God to search your heart today and show you anywhere pride is taking root.

Dig Deeper

Psalm 32:1
Ephesians 1:3–14
Proverbs 21:24

DAY 23

Woman with the Issue of Blood

"Who touched my clothes?" Jesus asked.

A moment earlier, He had been at the center of a huge crowd, each man and woman jostling to get just a little closer to the Miracle Worker as He made His way to Jairus's home so He might heal the synagogue ruler's daughter who lay dying.

Then, Jesus stopped, bringing the whole procession to a halt.

His disciples, exasperated at His delay, rolled their eyes at His ridiculous question.

"You see the people crowding against you," they responded, "and yet you can ask, 'Who touched me?'"

But Jesus knew. Something remarkable had just happened, but . . . the work was unfinished. Slowly, He scanned the crowd. Searching.

Searching for her.

She cowered as her heart pounded in her ears. Desperately, she tried to pull back to hide at the edges of the crowd to avoid His gaze. But it was relentless. With a sigh of despair, she realized that there was no use hiding.

Trembling, she pushed her way to the front of the throng to fall at His feet. Then, in front of appalled neighbors and strangers alike, she told Him the truth.

It was her. It was her body that had been restored, her unclean fingers that brushed the fringe of His prayer shawl. Then, she braced for the shame and judgment that she was certain would follow.

Instead, His voice softened, and He tenderly called her "daughter."

Daughter?

In shock, she lifted her eyes from the dust to find His and saw only love there. Love calling her from the shadows. Love calling her out of her shame.

No judgment. Only a blessing . . .

"Go in peace," He told her, "and be freed from your suffering."

And she rose twice healed—her body whole and her shame drowned in the sea of God's grace.

Scripture Reading

Read the passage below to learn more about the unusual way the woman with the hemorrhaging disease found healing.

Mark 5:21–34 NIV

When Jesus had again crossed over by boat to the other side of the lake, a large crowd gathered around Him while He was by the lake. Then one of the synagogue leaders, named Jairus, came, and when he saw Jesus, he fell at His feet. He pleaded earnestly with Him, "My little daughter is dying. Please come and put Your hands on her so that she will be healed and live." So Jesus went with him.

A large crowd followed and pressed around Him. And a woman was there who had been subject to bleeding for twelve years. She had suffered a great deal under the care of many doctors and had spent all she had, yet instead of getting better she grew worse. When she heard about Jesus, she came up behind Him in the crowd and touched His cloak, because she thought, "If I just touch His clothes, I will be healed." Immediately her bleeding stopped and she felt in her body that she was freed from her suffering.

At once Jesus realized that power had gone out from Him. He turned around in the crowd and asked, "Who touched My clothes?"

"You see the people crowding against You," His disciples answered, "and yet You can ask, 'Who touched Me?' "

But Jesus kept looking around to see who had done it. Then the woman, knowing what had happened to her, came and fell at His feet and, trembling with fear, told Him the whole truth. He said to her, "Daughter, your faith has healed you. Go in peace and be freed from your suffering."

Let's Review

When the woman in today's reading thinks, "If I just touch His clothes, I will be healed," she reveals the depth of her desperation to be made whole. Where in your life do you feel desperate for a "healing" from God? (This is not limited to physical healing.)

Jesus stops everything to seek out this woman and meet her face to face after her healing, revealing that she is a priority to Him. What do the disciples say to this? How does their reaction contrast that of Jesus?

Jesus calls the terrified woman "daughter" and tells her to "go in peace and be freed from your suffering." Do you, or someone dear to you, need to hear these words as well? Describe the situation below as well as your hope for God's intervention.

Application

How often does shame keep us from both God and each other?

It is a conflict as old as time. We first see the dynamic at play in the Garden of Eden, riding in on the back of the curse of sin. Adam and Eve feel shame and hide from God. God confronts their sin, at which point Adam blames Eve, building a wall of shame between him and his wife. (Genesis 3)

The woman in today's reading struggled physically for twelve years with a hemorrhaging disease, but her suffering was not limited to her body. Since her bleeding made her unclean according to Jewish religious law, she endured crushing isolation, and undoubtedly, the speculative condemnation of her neighbors who likely assumed her ailment was God's judgment for some secret sin.

One can only imagine the desperation that drove her from her home and into the crowded streets to defile a Rabbi with her very touch.

When Jesus realizes that power has gone out of Him because she touched the hem of His garment, He stops everything to call her from the edges of society, bound by shame, and back into her community, fully restored.

The woman is terrified, rightly assuming that the common response from a Rabbi in this situation would have been a harsh one. But not Jesus. He calls her "daughter," honors her faith, and then releases her to re-enter her life, healed both externally and internally.

Jesus is still calling us out of the shadows of shame and blame. He challenges us to hold each other in a greater grace and to meet our own faults and failings with self-compassion.

So, draw near to Him today. Like the woman in our reading, push past the dark clouds of shame that keep you isolated, weak, and weary. Reach out for Jesus and find that His love and grace are mightier than you could ever imagine.

go in peace & be free

Prompt

What holds you in the bondage of shame? Write a prayer asking God to set you free and bring healing to the depths of your soul.

Dig Deeper

Romans 8:1
Psalm 25:20
Galatians 5:1

DAY 24

Martha, Sister of Mary

Martha was . . . anxious.

Each day, she rose from her sleeping mat to undertake countless chores. Striving and serving. Working and worrying. Running and running in pursuit of worth.

Yes, Martha was anxious. Anxious and exhausted.

Now, here she was, her house full to overflowing with Jesus and His disciples, and there was more to do than ever.

Bread to bake.

Dishes to wash.

Vegetables to chop and meat to roast.

Frantically, her brow creased with tension, she bustled about her kitchen, occasionally glancing to where Mary sat in the place of a disciple (like a man!) at the feet of Jesus. With each hour that passed, Martha grew more and more anxious and eventually . . . *angry*.

Suddenly, before she even quite knew what was happening, she had interrupted Jesus's lesson to demand that He send Mary back to the kitchen where she belonged.

To her place.

Because nothing is more offensive to the bound than one who is free.

"Lord, don't you care that my sister has left me to do the work by myself? Tell her to help me!"

The room grew awkwardly quiet in the wake of her outburst. Jesus turned to her, searching her flushed and worry-lined face. She was so tired. So weary.

"Martha, Martha," the Lord answered, "you are worried and upset about many things, but few things are needed—or indeed only one. Mary has chosen what is better, and it will not be taken away from her."

Scripture Reading

Read the passage below for the scriptural account of Jesus's visit with Mary and Martha.

Luke 10:38–42 NIV

As Jesus and His disciples were on their way, He came to a village where a woman named Martha opened her home to Him. She had a sister called Mary, who sat at the Lord's feet listening to what He said. But Martha was distracted by all the preparations that had to be made. She came to Him and asked, "Lord, don't you care that my sister has left me to do the work by myself? Tell her to help me!"

"Martha, Martha," the Lord answered, "you are worried and upset about many things, but few things are needed—or indeed only one. Mary has chosen what is better, and it will not be taken away from her."

Let's Review

To "sit at the feet" of a rabbi meant to study under him as a disciple. Does it surprise you that Jesus defended Mary's right to study as a disciple, a role that was uncommon for a woman in her culture? Why or why not?

Martha felt a responsibility to correct Mary's behavior. Where in your life are you attempting to exert control over another person's choices, forfeiting your joy in the process?

Jesus said that when Mary chose studying instead of serving, she chose "what is better." How does this challenge you?

Application

A quick search of the internet concerning the health and well-being of modern-day workers reveals a disturbing truth: today's workforce is burned out and *absolutely exhausted*.

It is easy to get caught up in our cultural addiction to productivity, believing that our worth is somehow tied to how much we do, give, and serve. This harried exhaustion even finds its way into the church where endless programs ask for our attention, hours, and efforts.

Martha knew this impulse all too well. When Jesus and His friends came to stay at her house, she jumped right into her role as the ultimate hostess—cooking, cleaning, and serving.

How it must have infuriated her that Mary stubbornly refused to join her in her disfunction, opting instead to sit at the feet of Jesus as one of His disciples. Martha was so confident of Mary's impropriety (after all, everyone knew that only men were disciples!) that she interrupted Jesus's teaching to order Him to send Mary back to the kitchen where she belonged!

Jesus graciously declined, defending Mary's right to her theological education. He lovingly told Martha that Mary had chosen what was best. In doing so, Jesus not only protected Mary, but He also kept the door open to a different way of living for Martha.

We aren't told how Martha responded to Jesus. It is safe to assume that she was shocked by His words and actions. But isn't it nice to imagine the possibility that she quietly took her seat at the feet of Jesus instead of returning to the exhaustion of service?

Let each of us ponder Jesus's words of life to Martha as we step out into a world that rewards productivity, and the exhaustion that accompanies it, above all else:

"Martha, Martha," the Lord answered, "you are worried and upset about many things, but few things are needed—or indeed only one."

Indeed, only one.

Make space for God today. Rest in His loving presence. God wants more for your life than exhaustion.

rest in His loving presence

Prompt

Have the distractions in your life crowded out your time with God? Take some time to prayerfully consider how you might make space for God.

Dig Deeper

Psalm 119:17–24
Psalm 63:1–8
Matthew 4:4

DAY 25

The Bent Woman Healed on the Sabbath

For eighteen long years, her entire world had been the dust at her feet. She did not see the sky or the treetops. She rarely even saw the faces of her children as they transformed from toddlers to men and women. Permanently bent forward at a ninety-degree angle, she saw dust, the refuse in the street, and her own feet grow old and wrinkled as she shuffled along awkwardly through her days.

Early on, she discovered that her misplaced center of gravity made it precariously easy to lose her balance and fall headfirst, and so she learned to hold a short cane in her hand. The cane helped with her balance but did little to ease her agony.

Slowly, torturously, she made her way to the synagogue for the Sabbath service, the cane in her hand thudding softly as she walked. When she finally reached the door to the synagogue and cautiously descended the three steps into the interior, she found the room was already packed.

The woman strained her neck to lift her head enough to scan for an empty seat on one of the stone benches along the wall. Slowly, wearily, she made her way toward it, past the stone columns and beyond the Seat of Moses in the center of the room where a young Rabbi had already taken His place. When she neared Him, she felt His eyes on her, but she dismissed the thought to stay focused only on the seat awaiting her.

At last, she reached it. She sat down heavily, and with an audible sigh, propped her cane in the corner before placing her elbows on her knees so that she might support the weight of her forehead with her hands.

The room quieted as the *hazan*, the synagogue ruler, retrieved the scroll and brought it forward to hand it to the Rabbi. The Rabbi paused for a moment, gazing down at the scroll in His lap before handing it back to the *hazan*.

He then stood and called her to Him. She was too stunned to disobey. Slowly, she stood and then shuffled to where He stood waiting for her.

"Woman," He said gently, "you are set free from your infirmity."

Immediately, she felt the muscles in her back loosen and soften as she rose to her full height for the first time in eighteen years. In an instant, the pain which had been her constant companion for so long was gone. She lifted her hands to heaven and began to shout praises to God for her deliverance as a gasp of amazement rippled through the crowd. The young Rabbi simply smiled, retook the scroll, and sat down to teach.

The *hazan*, however, was incensed. Furiously, he turned to the woman and the crowd and began reprimanding them.

"There are six days for work. So come and be healed on those days, not on the Sabbath."

A few religious leaders who were present solemnly nodded their agreement.

Jesus turned toward them, His eyes flashing with anger.

"You hypocrites! Doesn't each of you on the Sabbath untie your ox or donkey from the stall and lead it out to give it water? Then should not this woman, a daughter of Abraham, whom Satan has kept bound for eighteen long years, be set free on the Sabbath day from what bound her?"

The crowd cheered as the religious leaders' faces flushed with embarrassment. The woman looked to the Savior and then back at the now useless cane in her hand. She laughed softly, shaking her head before lifting her tear-stained face to heaven once again.

"Hallelujah . . ." she whispered as the cane dropped from her fingers and clattered onto the stone floor at the feet of Jesus.

Scripture Reading

Read Luke's account of Jesus's healing of the bent woman on the Sabbath.

Luke 13:10–17 NIV

On a Sabbath Jesus was teaching in one of the synagogues, and a woman was there who had been crippled by a spirit for eighteen years. She was bent over and could not straighten up at all. When Jesus saw her, He called her forward and said to her, "Woman, you are set free from your infirmity." Then He put His hands on her, and immediately she straightened up and praised God.

Indignant because Jesus had healed on the Sabbath, the synagogue leader said to the people, "There are six days for work. So come and be healed on those days, not on the Sabbath."

The Lord answered him, "You hypocrites! Doesn't each of you on the Sabbath untie your ox or donkey from the stall and lead it out to give it water? Then should not this woman, a daughter of Abraham, whom Satan has kept bound for eighteen long years, be set free on the Sabbath day from what bound her?"

When He said this, all His opponents were humiliated, but the people were delighted with all the wonderful things He was doing.

Let's Review

In today's reading, the religious leaders had become so caught up in "what was right" that they neglected to love their neighbors. Where have you seen this same dynamic at play either in your faith community or culture at large?

The woman in today's story must have been shocked to have Rabbi Jesus notice her. Is there someone in your life who feels "unseen?" How might you offer them Jesus's love and compassion today?

The last verse of our reading describes the common people as being "delighted" with all Jesus was doing. Think about what you have learned about the religious leaders of Jesus's day through this study. Why do you think Jesus's teaching was so refreshing to the people?

Application

It is so easy to get caught up in being right that sometimes we forget to be loving.

If we are honest, perhaps this is because focusing on a strict list of dos and don'ts, dividing up the saints and the sinners, allows us to feel self-satisfied and superior. On the contrary, Jesus's challenge to love our neighbors as ourselves (Matthew 19:19) shifts our focus away from how other people are living to shine the bright light of His righteousness on our *own* hearts and the dark, selfish impulses that lie within.

In today's reading, Jesus unflinchingly confronted the hypocrisy He saw in the religious leaders of His day. He not only healed a woman on the Sabbath (a huge sin as far as they were concerned), *but He did so while teaching in the synagogue!*

His message to them, and to us, is clear: if our religion fails to notice the "least of these" and treat them with compassion, we have tragically missed what matters to the heart of God.

May we daily examine our hearts before God, asking Him to reveal to us where we have failed to fulfill the law of love. Then, with humble hands outstretched to heaven, ask Him to change us and give us a heart like His.

keep my

tender heart

Prompt

Write a prayer asking God to keep your heart tender toward those who are struggling.

Dig Deeper

Matthew 9:12–13
Matthew 23:23
I Peter 3:8

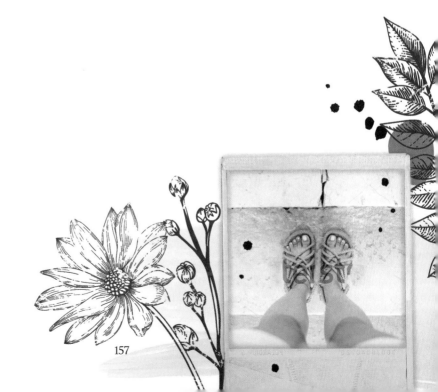

DAY 26

The Woman at the Well

When she stepped into the streets of Sychar, the midday heat took her breath away. The woman lifted her left hand to shield her eyes from the sun's glare and wrapped her right arm around the water jar that was braced against her hip. Then, with her eyes on the path before her, she quickly walked toward the well just beyond the city walls.

All the other women of Sychar had made the journey to draw water earlier that morning, as they did every day. It was much better to get the chore out of the way before the sun climbed too high in the sky. They made the journey to the well together for both companionship and safety. She was not part of their group. Her bad reputation had pushed her to the fringes of her community.

And so, she made the journey to the well in the heat of the day, rejected and alone.

Moments later, she lifted her eyes to the well in the distance and found, to her surprise, a man sitting on the edge of it. A few steps closer and it became apparent that it was a Jewish man. She groaned in frustration. She dealt with enough judgment from her own people . . .

the last thing she needed was a Jewish man looking down on her. She sighed in resignation, expecting Him to move out of the way of an "unclean woman."

But, He didn't. He not only remained stubbornly in her way—He spoke to her!

"Give me a drink," He said. A drink? She almost laughed out loud. "How is it that you, a Jew, ask a drink of me, a woman of Samaria?" she asked. When she voiced her curiosity to Him, the situation only grew more bizarre. He informed her that if she knew with Whom she was speaking, she would have asked Him for a drink and that He would have given her "living water."

Ridiculous. This man didn't even have a bucket.

"Are you greater than our father, Jacob?" she asked in exasperation. "This is his well, and he gave it to us Samaritans."

The Rabbi wasn't daunted by her argument. "Everyone who drinks of this water will be thirsty again," Jesus said, "but whoever drinks the water I give them will never thirst. Indeed, the water I give them will become in them a spring of water welling up to eternal life" (John 4:13–14 NIV).

If only, she thought. What a gift it would be to never thirst again.

"Then, give me some of this water, Sir," she responded wearily. "There is nothing I would love more than to no longer come to this well."

The Rabbi's eyes softened. This woman before Him was bound by shame, and her heart had been wounded beyond anything any woman should ever have to bear. Gently, He uncovered the source of her wound. "Go, call your husband and come back," He said.

She winced. How many men had used her and left her? Taken what they wanted and left nothing but shame and heartbreak in their wake? How could He know the source of her shame?

The conversation deepened as the woman and Jesus discussed differences of faith between Samaritans and Jews. "I know Messiah will come," she said to Him. "When He does, He will explain all of these things to us."

Jesus replied, "I, the one speaking to you—I am He."

She stared at Him in wonder until her reverie was broken by the sound of a group of men approaching. She glanced over her shoulder to find them regarding her and Jesus with obvious bewilderment. They were as confused by Jesus's treatment of her as she was.

Moments later, she stood in the streets of Sychar once again, now bustling with activity after the noon rest. She knew she had to tell her neighbors about the Man at the well. How better to get their attention than leverage her tarnished reputation?

"Come!" she called to her neighbors, "there is a Man at the well, and He told me everything I have ever done. Could this be the Messiah?"

Scripture Reading

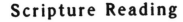

Read John's account of Jesus' conversation with the Samaritan woman at the well.

John 4:5–30, 39–42 NRSVA

[Jesus] came to a Samaritan city called Sychar ... Jacob's well was there, and Jesus, tired out by His journey, was sitting by the well. It was about noon.

A Samaritan woman came to draw water, and Jesus said to her, "Give Me a drink." (His disciples had gone to the city to buy food.) The Samaritan woman said to Him, "How is it that You, a Jew, ask a drink of me, a woman of Samaria?" (Jews do not share things in common with Samaritans.) Jesus answered her, "If you knew the gift of God and who it is that is saying to you, 'Give Me a drink,' you would have asked Him, and He would have given you living water." The woman said to Him, "Sir, You have no bucket, and the well is deep. Where do You get that living water? Are You greater than our ancestor Jacob, who gave us the well and with his sons and his flocks drank from it?" Jesus said to her, "Everyone who drinks of this water will be thirsty again, but those who drink of the water that I will give them will never be thirsty. The water that I will give will become in them a spring of water gushing up to eternal life." The woman said to Him, "Sir, give me this water, so that I may never be thirsty or have to keep coming here to draw water."

Jesus said to her, "Go, call your husband, and come back." The woman answered Him, "I have no husband." Jesus said to her, "You are right in saying, 'I have no husband,' for you have had five husbands, and the one you have now is not your husband. What you have said is true!" The woman said to Him, "Sir, I see that You are a prophet. Our ancestors worshiped on this mountain, but You say that the place where people must worship is in Jerusalem." Jesus said to her, "Woman, believe Me, the hour is coming when you will worship the Father neither on this mountain nor in Jerusalem. You worship what you do not know; we worship what we know, for salvation is from the Jews. But the hour is coming and is now here when the true worshippers will worship the Father in spirit and truth, for the Father seeks such as these to worship Him. God is spirit, and those who worship Him must worship in spirit and truth." The woman said to Him, "I know that Messiah is coming" (who is called Christ). "When He comes, He will proclaim all things to us." Jesus said to her, "I am He, the one who is speaking to you."

Just then His disciples came. They were astonished that He was speaking with a woman, but no one said, "What do you want?" or, "Why are you speaking with her?" Then the woman left her water-jar and went back to the city. She said to the people, "Come and see a man who told me everything I have ever done! He cannot be the Messiah, can He?"

Let's Review

In today's reading, Jesus turns upside down what many of us were taught about who is worthy to serve as a messenger of God. He didn't choose the most upstanding citizen in Sychar to bring the entire town to His saving truth. He chose the woman with the worst reputation. How does this challenge your expectations concerning who is worthy to speak into your life concerning spiritual matters?

Women during this time did not enjoy equal status with men and were, therefore, highly dependent upon them for protection and provision. Each time this woman was abandoned by her male protectors, her situation grew more precarious and her options more limited. How does Jesus's honoring and gentle interactions with her encourage you about His concern for your own wounds?

What implications do you imagine there were for this woman as far as her standing in her community when Jesus chose her as His spokesperson to the citizens of Sychar? Do you think her neighbors might have seen her in a more respectable light? Why or why not?

Application

Jesus frequently warned us in Scripture to abstain from judging each other, but it is a lesson many of us are slow to learn. Perhaps the cruelest judgments are those rendered for the wounds suffered by another.

It is easy to stand on the outside of loss and speculate who is to blame. Maybe we are tempted to do this because if the sufferer is to blame, then we might be able to avoid the same fate. Perhaps, in these situations, judgment provides us with the false comfort that we have some power to avoid suffering.

How would our worship communities and our families change if we considered the sufferer to hold a special place as one who has heard from God instead? What if we turned toward them in humility to receive from them what they learned from God in their darkest hour instead of turning away in judgment?

Psalm 34:18 (NRSVA) tells us, "The LORD is near to the broken-hearted, and saves the crushed in spirit." Furthermore, the story of Job offers us the hope that a season of incredible suffering is one in which God reveals deep truths to us.

At the end of the book of Job, after Job has weathered his season of suffering and heard from God in it, he says this of the Almighty:

> *"I had heard of You by the hearing of the ear,*
> *but now my eye sees You"* (Job 42:5 NRSVA).

An eye that has *seen* God. An ear that has heard Him speak in the darkest hour . . .

Who better to teach us than one who, like Job, has suffered?

May we abandon our fleshly desire for judgment to receive a glimpse of who God is to the sufferer. He is speaking through unlikely messengers. May we forever find ourselves willing to listen.

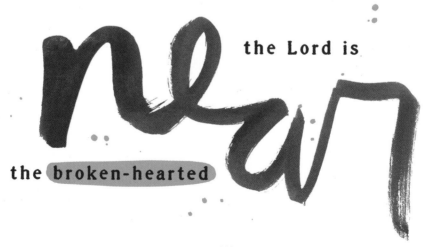

the Lord is near the broken-hearted

Prompt

At some point in your walk with Christ, have you passed unfair judgment on a member of your worship community? If so, take a moment to ask Him for His forgiveness in the space below. If not, write about how you might better love your brothers and sisters in Christ.

Dig Deeper

Isaiah 55:1–13
Matthew 8:5–13
John 1:11–13

DAY 27

The Adulteress

She couldn't stop shaking.

The woman stood in the temple courts, her eyes on the ground at her feet. Before her sat a Rabbi, the one they called "Jesus." He too had His eyes to the ground.

But not the other men—the men who had dragged her through the city streets, gathering a frenzied mob in their wake and forced her to stand beneath the weight of their accusations in the temple courts. Those men didn't grant her the mercy of their averted gazes. No, their eyes, filled with condemnation, never left her.

One of her accusers broke the silence to address Rabbi Jesus.

"Teacher, this woman was caught in the very act of committing adultery . . ."

Her heartbeat thundered in her ears, and she struggled to remain standing as her knees buckled beneath her. Still, she kept her eyes downward.

Dust on the tiles of the Court of Women. The filth of Jerusalem on her bare feet. The sand of Israel, crushed as fine as her own dignity, clinging to the hem of her tattered robe.

Oh, how she wished the earth would swallow her into its depths. Then, perhaps, she might be free of her shame.

Her accuser continued, his voice louder now. "In the law Moses commanded us to stone such women. Now what do You say?"

She held her breath, awaiting Jesus's judgment. Instead, He bent over and began to trace His finger through the dust at her feet, remaining silent as the men shouted over each other, each demanding He answer their question.

Finally, Jesus sat up, looked at the men and said, "Let anyone among you who is without sin be the first to throw a stone at her."

Then, He bent over and went back to writing in the dust. The men surrounding her fell into an awkward silence as they pondered His answer. Then, one by one, they wandered away until she was left alone with Jesus.

He sat up, dusted off His hands, and addressed her, His voice low and soft.

"Woman, where are they? Has no one condemned you?"

She stifled a sob, then lifted her tear-streaked face to gaze into His eyes.

"No one, Sir," she said.

"Neither do I condemn you," Jesus said.

She glanced back down at her dirty feet and the dust of Jerusalem on the tiles of the temple courts. Miraculously, not only did the earth still hold firm beneath her, but she had also been freed of her shame.

"Go your way," Jesus said gently, "and from now on do not sin again."

Scripture Reading

Read the passage below for the account of Jesus' forgiveness, and deliverance, of a woman who was caught in adultery.

John 8:2–11 NRSVA

Early in the morning He came again to the temple. All the people came to Him, and He sat down and began to teach them. The scribes and the Pharisees brought a woman who had been caught in adultery; and making her stand before all of them, they said to Him, "Teacher, this woman was caught in the very act of committing adultery. Now in the law Moses commanded us to stone such women. Now what do You say?" They said this to test Him, so that they might have some charge to bring against Him. Jesus bent down and wrote with His finger on the ground. When they kept on questioning Him, He straightened up and said to them, "Let anyone among you who is without sin be the first to throw a stone at her." And once again He bent down and wrote on the ground. When they heard it, they went away, one by one, beginning with the elders, and Jesus was left alone with the woman standing before Him. Jesus straightened up and said to her, "Woman, where are they? Has no one condemned you?" She said, "No one, Sir." And Jesus said, "Neither do I condemn you. Go your way, and from now on do not sin again."

Let's Review

The religious leaders met the woman's sin with shame and condemnation. Jesus, however, not only offered her grace, but He was also careful to preserve her dignity.

In your experience, do our faith communities respond to sin more like the woman's accusers or like Jesus?

In Jesus's day, any woman caught in the "very act of adultery," especially one drug into the temple courts to face judgment, would have felt unbearable shame.

When you have fallen into sin, do you find that feelings of shame make it difficult for you to approach God for forgiveness? Why or why not?

How does Jesus's treatment of the woman in today's story bring you comfort and encouragement?

Application

Jesus never shied away from challenging the religious leaders of His day. He pushed against their flawed doctrines until they crumbled. He leveled their edifice of religiosity, built stone by stone upon their declarations of who was acceptable to God and who wasn't, to lay a new foundation of mercy and grace in its place.

Jesus was a friend to the "sinners" they shunned. He offered His healing touch to the very people they crossed the street to avoid, and He granted dignity and forgiveness to those they condemned and shamed.

The woman in today's reading was one of those. At first glance, it might appear that this group of religious leaders are performing a public service by rooting out immorality and holding the good people of Jerusalem to a high standard of holy living.

When we dig a little deeper, however, we are left with important questions such as:

If this woman was caught in the "very act of adultery," where was the man with whom she committed her offense? Why was she the only one brought forward for judgment?

And, why were they bringing her to Jesus? Was this more about them attempting to trap Jesus in a doctrinal quagmire than it was about this woman's sin?

Most importantly, why does Jesus behave the way He does and say the things He says?

The story of Jesus's gentle mercy and gracious pardon of this woman challenges us to search our own lives to determine whom we most resemble of those present that day. Unfortunately, very few of us can claim to reflect Jesus. Most of us are either the woman, bound by sin and hopeless in shame, or the men who mercilessly condemned her.

Jesus once proclaimed that there were no greater commandments than those to love God and love our neighbor. So simple, but far from easy. When we love God and love our neighbor, we are forced to discard our list of rights and wrongs that allow us to feel superior, and instead accept the truth that we aren't better than anyone else. We are all just sinners saved by grace.

Today, may we all ask Jesus to give us eyes to see not only our own sin but also our neighbors' sin as He does—through the eyes of gentle grace and tender love.

gentle grace & tender love

Prompt

Does shame stalk you today? Bring it to God. Ask Him to forgive your sin and set your heart at peace.

Dig Deeper

Psalm 40:11
Isaiah 30:18
Psalm 23:2–3

DAY 28

Mary, Sister of Lazarus

Mary was lost in the timelessness of grief. How many days had passed since she and her sister, Martha, sent word to Jesus that their brother, Lazarus, was gravely ill?

How long since they laid Lazarus in the tomb?

With tremendous difficulty, Mary pushed her brain to remember until, at last, the information rose to the surface.

It was the fourth day. The sorrowful, terribly final, fourth day since they buried Lazarus. Jewish tradition held that the soul remained near the body for three days after death, offering the bereaved a thin thread of hope that their loved one might still return to life.

But now, all hope was gone.

Losing Lazarus was an overwhelming grief, but there was another sorrow beneath it . . .

Jesus hadn't come when they called for Him. He tarried for two long days before beginning His journey to Bethany as Lazarus struggled for breath. Two precious days in which He might have restored their brother to health.

Why hadn't He answered when they called? Why had He delayed His coming?

Just then, Martha walked into the room and took Mary's hands in her own.

"The Teacher is here," she said, "and is asking for you."

Without a word, Mary leapt to her feet and ran to meet Him.

Minutes later, she was falling at His feet, weeping, pouring out her grief for Lazarus and her heartbreak over Jesus's silence in the moment she needed Him most.

"Lord, if you had been here," she cried, "my brother would not have died."

Through His own tears, Jesus simply asked, "Where have you laid him?"

A moment later, Jesus stood before the tomb and ordered the stone rolled away from the entrance. Martha, ever practical, moved to stop Him.

"Did I not tell you," He asked in response, "that if you believe, you will see the glory of God?"

Then, after taking a moment to pray, Jesus shouted, "Lazarus, come out!"

And . . . there he was! Wrapped head to toe in burial clothes, standing at the entrance of the tomb. Mary cried out in wonder and joy. Lazarus was alive!

Beside her, Jesus smiled through His tears, "Take off the grave clothes," He said, "and let him go."

Scripture Reading

Read the passage below to learn more about how Jesus responded to Mary's heartbreak over the death of her brother Lazarus.

John 11:32–44 NIV

When Mary reached the place where Jesus was and saw Him, she fell at His feet and said, "Lord, if You had been here, my brother would not have died."

When Jesus saw her weeping, and the Jews who had come along with her also weeping, He was deeply moved in spirit and troubled. "Where have you laid him?" He asked.

"Come and see, Lord," they replied.

Jesus wept.

Then the Jews said, "See how He loved him!"

But some of them said, "Could not He who opened the eyes of the blind man have kept this man from dying?"

Jesus, once more deeply moved, came to the tomb. It was a cave with a stone laid across the entrance. "Take away the stone," He said.

"But, Lord," said Martha, the sister of the dead man, "by this time there is a bad odor, for he has been there four days."

Then Jesus said, "Did I not tell you that if you believe, you will see the glory of God?"

So they took away the stone. Then Jesus looked up and said, "Father, I thank You that You have heard Me. I knew that You always hear Me, but I said this for the benefit of the people standing here, that they may believe that You sent Me."

When He had said this, Jesus called in a loud voice, "Lazarus, come out!" The dead man came out, his hands and feet wrapped with strips of linen, and a cloth around his face.

Jesus said to them, "Take off the grave clothes and let him go."

Let's Review

Imagine that you are Mary watching Lazarus grow increasingly ill, awaiting Jesus's arrival. What emotions would you experience? How would Jesus's apparent procrastination challenge your faith in Him?

When Mary falls at Jesus's feet, she doesn't hold back in expressing her hurt and disappointment. Why do you think it is so important to be unflinchingly honest with God when we are hurting the most?

When Jesus delayed His coming, Mary must have doubted His love for her.
Think for a moment about the portion of our reading that describes Jesus's response when faced with Mary's grief. What does this tell you about God's heart for His children when they are suffering?

Application

If you walk with Jesus long enough, the moment will come when it feels as if He is stubbornly silent in the face of your pain. When this happens, your most fervent, faith-filled prayers will eventually give way to the psalmist's cry:

"How long, O Lord?" (Psalm 13:1 NIV).

It is almost impossible to imagine how acutely Mary must have felt this deep lament. As a close friend of Jesus, she had witnessed Jesus do incredible things. She possessed absolute confidence that He could heal her beloved brother.

But instead of coming quickly to do so, He delayed His coming until He knew it was too late to save Lazarus.

Mary was, understandably, crushed.

There are many gifts in her story. In reading it, we are moved by Jesus's deep compassion for the grieving as He weeps alongside them. We are thrilled by His awesome power as He summons Lazarus, still bound in grave clothes, from the tomb after four days dead.

But perhaps, the sweetest gift is the permission God gives us through Mary's example to express our disappointment and hurt to Him honestly.

As we carry tender hearts through a sin-scarred world, there will be painful seasons in which it feels as if God's answer to our cries for help are unreasonably delayed. When this happens, we must lean hard on the truths revealed to us in today's story:

God is good.

He is loving.

And He is able to do more than we could ever ask or imagine (Ephesians 3:20 NIV).

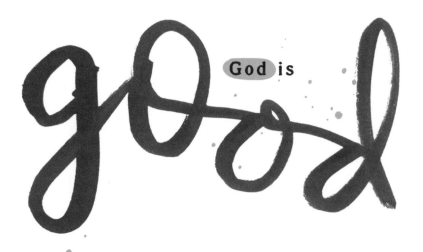

God is good

Prompt

Where do you need God's miraculous resurrection power in your life today?

Take a moment to honestly express your longing for deliverance to Him.

Dig Deeper

Psalm 22:1–5
Luke 18:6–8
Matthew 7:7–10

DAY 29

Mary, Mother of Jesus, at the Cross

My boy . . .

My boy . . .

Oh, God help me, my precious boy . . .

Mary stood as near to Jesus's cross as she could, longing to reach out her hand to touch Him and bring Him some small comfort. In horror, she had borne witness to each lash of the whip as it fell against His back, every strike of the hammer as it drove the cruel iron nail through His wrists and ankles.

Now, as she watched Him struggle against the nails to push Himself high enough to catch a brief gasp of air before sinking down again in agony and exhaustion, the words Simeon spoke over her on the day of newborn Jesus's presentation at the temple came back to her.

"And a sword will pierce your own soul too" (Luke 2:35 NIV).

A chill had passed through her at the words, prompting her to protectively pull her baby closer to her chest. Now, her baby was suffering, and dying, on a Roman cross.

Mary bowed her head, covered her face with her hands, and sobbed.

The sound of Jesus struggling to push Himself upward again prompted her to look up. His eyes, swollen and caked with blood, were on her. He gasped and turned His head to where John stood next to her.

"Woman," He said to her, "here is your son."

Then to John, "Here is your mother."

He sank down once again, His face contorted in pain, but His eyes, filled with love and sorrow, lingered on hers. From His cross, Jesus had ensured that she would be well-cared for after His death.

The tears flowed down Mary's face. Oh, how she longed to return to the time when she could still pull Him close and keep Him safe.

John moved a step closer to her, comforting her with his presence even as his own heart was breaking.

They would keep vigil at Jesus's side until the very end . . .

Scripture Reading

Read the Scripture below for the account of Jesus' loving care for His mother as she stood vigil at the foot of His cross.

John 19:16–27 NIV

Finally, Pilate handed Him over to them to be crucified.

So the soldiers took charge of Jesus. Carrying His own cross, He went out to the place of the Skull (which in Aramaic is called Golgotha). There they crucified Him, and with Him two others—one on each side and Jesus in the middle.

Pilate had a notice prepared and fastened to the cross. It read: JESUS OF NAZARETH, THE KING OF THE JEWS. Many of the Jews read this sign, for the place where Jesus was crucified was near the city, and the sign was written in Aramaic, Latin and Greek. The chief priests of the Jews protested to Pilate, "Do not write 'The King of the Jews,' but that this man claimed to be king of the Jews."

Pilate answered, "What I have written, I have written."

When the soldiers crucified Jesus, they took His clothes, dividing them into four shares, one for each of them, with the undergarment remaining. This garment was seamless, woven in one piece from top to bottom.

"Let's not tear it," they said to one another. "Let's decide by lot who will get it."

This happened that the Scripture might be fulfilled that said,

"They divided My clothes among them
    and cast lots for My garment."

So this is what the soldiers did.

Near the cross of Jesus stood His mother, His mother's sister, Mary the wife of Clopas, and Mary Magdalene. When Jesus saw His mother there, and the disciple whom He loved standing nearby, He said to her, "Woman, here is your son," and to the disciple, "Here is your mother." From that time on, this disciple took her into his home.

Let's Review

What does Jesus's prioritizing of Mary's comfort and care tell you about how much your temporal, physical needs matter to an infinite, eternal God?

Jesus prayed ceaselessly throughout His ministry. It is safe to assume that He continued to do so even as He hung from His cross. What do you think He might have been praying for His mother and friends?

If Jesus took the time to care for His mother's physical needs while undertaking the work of redemption, what implication does that have for us as we serve as His hands and feet in a hurting world?

179

Application

It is impossible for most of us to imagine what it must have been like for Mary to watch her firstborn Son suffer flogging and crucifixion. She must have begged God to spare Him—bargained hard with heaven to take Her boy's place.

But the work of salvation belonged to Jesus alone. Mary could stay near, but there was little she could do to offer Him comfort or relief. She, who had carried Him in her womb, faithfully nurtured Him into adulthood, and now stood vigil at His cross, could not walk alongside Him on the dark path of suffering and death that lay before Him.

It must have been torture for her.

Remarkably, Jesus made it a priority to do what He could to relieve her acute suffering by entrusting her into John's care. He wasn't too busy with the redemption of creation to comfort His mom.

Today's reading shows us that while God is deeply concerned about the "big issues," our day-to-day needs also matter to Him. The vast love of God for us is stunning. Awe-inspiring. Inexhaustible.

Poet and physician Oliver Wendell Holmes Sr. once said, "Some people are so heavenly minded that they are no earthly good." Jesus never lost sight of or belittled the struggles and sorrows of the people who crossed His path during His ministry. May the tender and personal love of God challenge us to love like He does. May we never be too busy, too caught up with illusions of our own importance, to offer compassion to a hurting world.

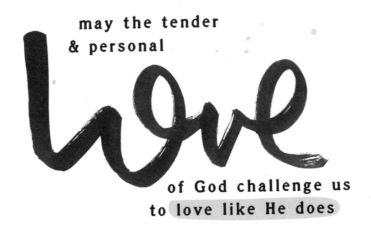

may the tender & personal *love* of God challenge us to love like He does

Prompt

Do you need Jesus's tender compassion today? Write a prayer pouring out your heartbreak to Him.

Dig Deeper

Psalm 138:6
Psalm 34:10
Matthew 25:35–40

DAY 30

Mary Magdalene, Messenger of the Good News

She stood at the door of the empty tomb, weeping.

She wasn't sure what to do. When she found that Jesus's body was missing, she had gone to Peter and John for help. They ran to the tomb, saw that the stone was rolled away and the grave cloths were discarded on the bench where the body had been, shook their heads in dismay, and returned home.

But she couldn't bring herself to leave, not while Jesus's body was still missing.

Once again, she bent over to peer into the tomb. To her shock, two men dressed in white were sitting on the bench where Jesus's body had lain.

"Woman," they asked, "why are you crying?"

Mary, numb with trauma and grief, responded through her tears.

"They have taken my Lord away," she said, "and I don't know where they have put Him."

At that, another man appeared behind her.

"Woman, why are you crying?" He asked. "Who is it you are looking for?"

It must be the gardener, she thought. Maybe he knows where the body is . . .

"Sir, if you have carried Him away, tell me where you have put Him, and I will get Him," she pleaded.

Then, tenderly, He said her name . . .

"Mary . . ."

Mary's eyes flew open with sudden recognition. *How could it be?*

Mary spun around to where Jesus stood behind her, fell to the ground, and grasped His feet in her hands.

"Rabboni!" she cried.

Jesus laughed softly. "Don't hold on to Me," He said, "for I have not yet ascended to the Father. Go instead to my brothers and tell them, 'I am ascending to My Father and your Father, to My God and your God.'"

With a cry of joy, Mary leapt to her feet to obey. Moments later, she burst through the door where the grieving disciples had gathered, ready to deliver the impossible, miraculous announcement that would change everything . . .

"I have seen the Lord!"

Scripture Reading

Read the passage below to learn more about how Mary Magdalene became the first to proclaim the good news of Jesus's resurrection.

John 20:3–18 NIV

So Peter and the other disciple started for the tomb. Both were running, but the other disciple outran Peter and reached the tomb first. He bent over and looked in at the strips of linen lying there but did not go in. Then Simon Peter came along behind him and went straight into the tomb. He saw the strips of linen lying there, as well as the cloth that had been wrapped around Jesus' head. The cloth was still lying in its place, separate from the linen. Finally the other disciple, who had reached the tomb first, also went inside. He saw and believed. (They still did not understand from Scripture that Jesus had to rise from the dead.) Then the disciples went back to where they were staying.

Now Mary stood outside the tomb crying. As she wept, she bent over to look into the tomb and saw two angels in white, seated where Jesus' body had been, one at the head and the other at the foot.

They asked her, "Woman, why are you crying?"

"They have taken my Lord away," she said, "and I don't know where they have put Him." At this, she turned around and saw Jesus standing there, but she did not realize that it was Jesus.

He asked her, "Woman, why are you crying? Who is it you are looking for?"

Thinking He was the gardener, she said, "Sir, if you have carried Him away, tell me where you have put Him, and I will get Him."

Jesus said to her, "Mary."

She turned toward Him and cried out in Aramaic, "Rabboni!" (which means "Teacher").

Jesus said, "Do not hold on to Me, for I have not yet ascended to the Father. Go instead to My brothers and tell them, 'I am ascending to My Father and your Father, to My God and your God.'"

Mary Magdalene went to the disciples with the news: "I have seen the Lord!" And she told them that He had said these things to her.

Let's Review

When Peter and John arrived at the tomb, it was empty except for the burial cloths. Why do you think Jesus waited to reveal Himself to Mary instead of Peter and John?

Mark 16:9 tells us that Jesus delivered Mary from demon possession—seven demons to be exact! Yet, He chose to honor her above all others by appearing to her first after His resurrection and commissioning her to carry the good news to His "brothers." Have you ever struggled with feeling as if you aren't qualified to be used by God? If so, how does Jesus's honoring of Mary, despite her past, encourage you?

It is clear from today's reading that Mary loved Jesus very much. Do you think this is why He revealed Himself to her first and made her His messenger? Why or why not?

Application

During the Rabbinical Period, women suffered tremendous losses to their status, and in some cases, their rights. One rabbi ruled that a man could divorce his wife if she "goes out with her hair unbound or spins in the street" (Mishnah: Ketuboth 7:6).

Jesus, however, honored women throughout His life. He came to earth through a virgin's womb, welcomed women as disciples, defended and protected them when they were under attack, and in today's story, honored a woman by appearing to her first after His resurrection and then commissioning her to carry the good news to His brothers.

As modern women, these might seem like small things, but rest assured that in the first century, they were nothing short of radical.

Mary Magdalene's story offers us this assurance: our love and devotion to God, along with our willingness to serve Him, are far more important to God than our status, gifts, or past.

Jesus is in the business of lifting women up, restoring them, and empowering them to do mighty works in His kingdom.

May we step boldly into His purpose for us, and with Mary, joyfully proclaim the good news of His resurrection: "I have seen the Lord!" (John 20:18 NIV).

I have seen the Lord

Prompt

Write a prayer thanking God for His great love for you.

Dig Deeper

Psalm 139:1–6
Psalm 139:7–12
Psalm 139:13–24

ABOUT THE AUTHOR

SHANNA NOEL *is the founder and owner of Illustrated Faith and the Bible-journaling community. Her other well-known devotional journals include* 100 Days of Bible Promises, 100 Days of Grace and Gratitude, *and* 100 Days of Less Hustle, More Jesus. *Shanna lives in the Pacific Northwest with her husband of twenty years, Jonathan, and their two daughters. When they aren't doing something creative as a family, you can find them playing a board game with a bowl of fresh popcorn and lots of laughs.*

ABOUT THE AUTHOR

SHERRI GRAGG *utilizes cultural background, and her unique style of storytelling, to immerse readers in some of the most riveting moments in Scripture. She is the author of five books including* Advent: The Story of Christmas *(Dayspring, 2019) and* Arms Open Wide: A Call to Linger in the Savior's Presence *(Thomas Nelson, 2016). Sherri is a nationally published freelance writer and mother of five children. She lives and writes in beautiful Franklin, Tennessee.*

For more from author Sherri Gragg, check out *Advent: The Story of Christmas.*

Available at **dayspring.com** as well as several retail stores near you.

Did you enjoy this devotional guide? If so, be sure to check out the first book in this series, *From Where I Stand: 30 Days in the Life of Paul.*

Available on **dayspring.com** as well as several retailers near you.